NINA KEEGAN

100 DAYS WITH GOD II

100 Devotions for Living a Victorious Life in Christ Jesus

Overwhelming victory is ours through Christ who loved us.
— Romans 8:37

Copyright © 2021 by Nina Keegan

ISBN 978-1-7355259-3-8

All rights reserved. No part of this book may be reproduced or used in any manner without the prior written permission of the copyright owner, except for the use of brief quotations in a book review.

This book does not replace the advice of a medical professional. Consult your physician before making any changes to your diet or regular health plan. The information in this book was correct at the time of publication, but the author does not assume any liability for loss or damage caused by errors or omissions.

"I highly recommend you read and dig into this powerful devotional. It will fan the flame of your faith and stir up your hunger even more to go deeper with the Father. Nina Keegan has a way with words that will transport you to the secret place and encounter the river of God's grace in a powerful way."

—Scott Nary
Founder of 420 Fire International

"I totally recommend this devotional! Nina has such great spiritual insights and practical application of the scriptures into our lives and situations. Reading this daily devotion every day will help you think through God's will for your life and how to walk worthy of His calling on your life. I praise God for Nina and this book to encourage others to do the work of the kingdom—to make disciples and share the gospel!"

—Pastor Chuck Reich
Host of *Answering the Call*

"I have walked with Nina on her journey with the Lord and she walks in miracles. She spends time in the presence of the Lord and this book makes that clear. At the end of 100 days, you will walk with Jesus in a much deeper way and will hear and recognize His voice which will lead you to major breakthroughs in your own life. You will not be able to put it down!"

—Michelle Humphreys
Co-host of *Grace Grace with Nina and Michelle*

Dedication

I would like to dedicate this book first and foremost to our loving Creator, God almighty...

THANK YOU for saving me... Thank you for finding me right where I was and loving me whole! Making your Son Jesus the Lord of my life was the most precious gift and the best decision I have ever made!

Thank you to my amazing husband, Richard. You are my rock. I am so grateful for your love and support. You have my whole heart! You are a godsend!

To my fabulous sons Kyle and Kristopher and my sweet daughter-in-law Brittany:

I love you all with my whole heart. I am so grateful that I get to do life with you all. I could not be prouder of the wonderful human beings you are! Thank you for always encouraging me! You are all true blessings. I learn from you all every day!

To my precious friend and cohost, Michelle Humphreys:

God sure knew what he was doing when he put you in my life... You are my family! There are many more God adventures to come!

To all of those who read, watch and follow my ministry:

You greatly encourage! I thank God for each and every one of you and pray for you daily! God bless you all!

Introduction

A life steeped in the goodness and the glory of God found only by seeking Him first will always result in a life that is exceedingly abundantly better than you could ever ask or think. Our lives can be naturally supernatural. When we set our minds and hearts to be Kingdom minded, the cares of this world will grow strangely dim.

All things pale in comparison to Almighty God. What can be better than His plan for our lives?

So many of us needlessly take the difficult path, trying to do things on our own. I know myself I've had to learn this lesson the hard way. Nothing can stop what God ordains. His plan for us is a divine blueprint of His love poured out upon us in pure perfection. The battles I have faced in my life have not always been easy. I have experienced much heartache and pain. But when I have let God lead in my life, the ultimate results have been miraculous breakthrough and overwhelming victory each and every time.

These entries are the wisdom of my past. It is God who has provided me with strength and boldness to step into my future knowing and understanding that He has already gone before me to make known His brilliant pathway and He has beautifully written a divine order for each step I will ever take.

When we set our minds on putting God first and seeking His plan for our lives, what results is better than we could ever hope for as Christians. I pray this book will fill you with peace. I pray it strengthens your faith and helps you live victoriously in Christ.

I pray you step out in faith and boldly live a life of unimaginable victory as you seek to navigate your path with Christ. Everything is better, everything is easier when we give it to God. Let's walk together with the Lord for 100 days!

Ephesians 3:20-21 states:

"Now all glory to God, who is able, through his mighty power at work within us, to accomplish infinitely more than we might ask or think. Glory to him in the church and in Christ Jesus through all generations forever and ever! Amen."

The verses shared in *100 Days with God II* are from the New Living Translation (NLT) version of the Bible.

God Restores What Is Broken

DAY 1

While reading the scriptures of Exodus, I found this statement: "God restores."

Yes, God restores! It is true in the story of Moses, as well as our own lives.

After working tirelessly to chisel the Ten Commandments on the granite tablets, Moses returned to find that the Israelites had grown tired of waiting for him and decided to create an idol, or false God, to worship.

In his outrage, Moses destroyed the stone tablets. But, as stated above, God restores what is broken.

Exodus 34:1 states:

> "THEN THE LORD TOLD MOSES, 'CHISEL OUT TWO STONE TABLETS LIKE THE FIRST ONES. I WILL WRITE ON THEM THE SAME WORDS THAT WERE ON THE TABLETS YOU SMASHED.'"

Yes, God would rewrite the same words! Even though the tablets were broken in anger, God still expedited the restoration; He did not make Moses labor and rewrite all the Commandments himself. There was such mercy and kindness in His restoration process.

God understands us: He knows we are human, He knows our flaws and our weaknesses, and He is so quick to forgive us all of our iniquities. What I love *most*, however, is that God goes one step further and personally restores us. We serve a good God, who sees all injustices, and who settles and solves the cases of His people.

I am reminded of the scripture in Ephesians 3:20:

"Now all glory to God, who is able, through his mighty power at work within us, to accomplish infinitely more than we might ask or think."

God will always restore!

To Obey or Not to Obey

DAY 2

To obey or disobey? Every day, we are faced with this choice.

While reading about the death of Saul in 1 Samuel 31, I realized that within it are two tales of obedience, intertwined: Both Saul and his armor bearer faced a choice.

Saul was self-serving, which made him small in God's eyes. Even though he was rich, he was spiritually bankrupt.

In the end, Saul knew that if the enemies captured him, he would suffer greatly, so he asked his armor bearer to kill him. Saul faced death the same way he faced life: He took matters into his own hands, without thinking of God or asking God for his guidance.

1 Samuel 31:4-6 states:

> "Saul groaned to his armor bearer, 'Take your sword and kill me before these pagan Philistines come to run me through and taunt and torture me.'
>
> But, his armor bearer was afraid and would not do it. So, Saul took his own sword and fell on it. When his armor bearer realized that Saul was dead, he fell on his own sword and died beside the king. So Saul, his three sons, his armor bearer, and his troops all died together that same day."

The armor bearer had a choice to make: He knew that if he would have slain Saul, he would have been disobedient to God. Instead, he chose to give his own mortal life for obedience and eternal life.

God loves obedience, especially when it is difficult. We must always have courage to follow God and His laws above anything earthly, even our own personal desires. This is the greatest defense against sin and temptation.

Ask God for revelation and for confirmation, and step out and do that which He has called you to do. I promise that you will be so glad you did!

Be Vigilant

DAY 3

We must be vigilant to stay on God's path! The enemy wants to trap us into settling for less than God's best. Satan would love nothing more than for us to be tricked and follow his path, disguised as that of God's.

1 Peter 5:8 warns:

> "STAY ALERT! WATCH OUT FOR YOUR GREAT ENEMY, THE DEVIL. HE PROWLS AROUND LIKE A ROARING LION, LOOKING FOR SOMEONE TO DEVOUR."

The enemy comes dressed as an angel of light; he knows the Word, and twists it to try and keep us from the peace, prosperity, and divine purpose that God has for us. But, God says that His sheep shall know His voice, and that there will always be confirmation and an absolute abundance of proof!

When God speaks, there is a great peace. God is the author and the finisher of our stories, and it is always for our own good. We can make our plans, but God will always order our steps. God allows us to face tests that stretch our faith, which causes us to repent and then turn to Him with our whole hearts.

Every day, we must surrender and trust God to never let us be deceived. We do not want to wander in the wilderness, or spend 40 years aimlessly searching for the gates to the promised land: We are going in now!

Wherever the enemy is operating in our lives, we should ask God to shine a great light on it, and to take the veils off our eyes so that we might see the enemy's plans. We must bind and sever every person, place, or thing that is being used in our lives as a hindrance to our blessings.

Let us have no fear of man; let us only have the fear of letting You down! We must remain vigilant and stay on the proper path!

Not Our Way, but Yours, God

DAY 4

"I don't care what anyone says! I'm going to do it!"

Does this sound familiar? The words change, but the essential message is always the same: A person is closed off to advice because his or her prideful mind is already made up.

Do we ever open our Bibles, asking God to show us a scripture, but when He shows us what seems to be a scripture of rebuke, or one of God gently presenting us with conviction, our tendency is to discount it immediately? We move on until we find one that suits exactly what we need to establish our own plan.

But, we must not let pride steal our destiny! A haughty attitude can lead to a pathway of destruction, and the enemy lurks in a prideful spirit. We must be very careful of this prideful tendency, so that we do not fall into our own trap by rejecting the wise counsel of others.

In Proverbs 11:14, it is written:

> "WITHOUT WISE LEADERSHIP, A NATION FALLS; THERE IS SAFETY IN HAVING MANY ADVISERS."

How can you prevent a life-changing mistake resulting from pride? Seek wise and Godly counsel from others whom you respect and trust, stay in the word of God and know it for yourself, pray fervently, worship Him, and seek His wisdom and peace for leadership in your life.

Know Who You Are in Christ

DAY 5

We must know our glorious Father in Heaven. We must whole-heartedly know that He is with us, even in difficult times. Remember, Jesus did not have an identity crisis: He went straight to the Father and prayed.

John 14:13-14 states:

> "YOU CAN ASK FOR ANYTHING IN MY NAME, AND I WILL DO IT, SO THAT THE SON CAN BRING GLORY TO THE FATHER. YES, ASK ME FOR ANYTHING IN MY NAME, AND I WILL DO IT!"

It is time to start asking and praying for protection against deception. The Bible tells us that, in the last days, we will be greatly deceived.

So many strong Christians are being deceived by others, even fellow Christians, saying, "Shouldn't we be more tolerant of other faiths? Shouldn't we be tolerant of other beliefs? Shouldn't we all just try to love one another for our differences?"

Yes, we are called to love everyone; it is a commandment. We are to love as God loves, even our enemies, but *not* for their differences. The enemy loves tolerance because tolerance does not spread the Gospel: Tolerance backs away. Tolerance is afraid of conflict. Tolerance is non-controversial.

This is no time to ride the fence and be double-minded! Tolerance, for the sake of tolerance, allows people to believe sin is okay, even if it goes against God's word. We must get on board with the Revival that God is stirring up in each of us. We must decide if we are going to accommodate the world and what is happening in it, or if we will refuse to compromise our beliefs and our behaviors and, instead, live in absolute the assuredness of following the Word of God.

No matter what is going on in the world, we must believe that the Body of Christ can rest assured, that He has never moved from His exalted seat. He has full power and authority, He holds us all in His hands, and He is fighting for us. The Gospel will prevail. The blood of Jesus is still speaking, as it always will. Know who you are in Christ!

Spring Cleaning

DAY 6

One spring, with great caution, I opened the door to my storage closet with the best of intentions of doing my "spring cleaning."

I took one look inside at the cardboard boxes, bags of who-knows-what, and a plethora of abandoned "tchotchkes" (you know, the things I haven't seen in a couple years, yet couldn't possibly live without), and overwhelmingly declared, "This is not happening today!"

I promptly closed the door. Out of sight, out of mind.

We tend to pack away things—things that we think we need to hold on to, "just in case." It is easy to become bogged down with weighty, old inventory. We stuff it and cram it down until the door can finally close it all off to the world.

Our minds are so much like those overstuffed and messy closets.

What do we stuff away in the deep closets of our thoughts? What is weighing down our hearts, our emotions, our souls? There is so much abandoned, but not forgotten. Our minds are often overflowing with pain, deep hurt, unforgiveness, regret, guilt, grief, and bitterness.

But, pain is the place where we can always meet authentically with God. He knows where you are, who has hurt you, and why, and He is *never* surprised by what is in your closet. We cannot hide anything from God.

2 Timothy 2:21 states:

"If you keep yourself pure, you will be a special utensil for honorable use. Your life will be clean, and you will be ready for the Master to use you for every good work."

It is time to clean house and let everything go. It is time to prioritize God over your pain. The Bible says we are to have and enjoy our lives every day, no matter what is going on. We can still experience joy with Jesus, regardless of our circumstances.

God wants to meet you right there in your closet. God wants to be the light in the darkness, and restore you on every level!

God Is Eager to Bless Us

DAY 7

In reading Haggai 2:19, I came across this scripture concerning the rebuilding of the Lord's Temple:

> "I AM GIVING YOU A PROMISE NOW, WHILE THE SEED IS STILL IN THE BARN. YOU HAVE NOT YET HARVESTED YOUR GRAIN, AND YOUR GRAPEVINES, FIG TREES, POMEGRANATES, AND OLIVE TREES HAVE NOT YET PRODUCED THEIR CROPS. BUT FROM THIS DAY ONWARD, I WILL BLESS YOU."

You see, once God's followers started to rebuild the foundation of the temple, God blessed them immediately. He did not wait for the project to be completed. The very minute we take steps of obedience in the right direction towards what God wants us to do, He sends his encouragement and His approval! God is so eager to bless us, even while our seed is still in the barn.

Our ability to be blessed depends on our obedience to the Lord, and what He is calling us to do. We cannot keep asking God to order our steps and put us in His plan if we are too lazy to move, or unwilling to listen to His word. If we want to be blessed, we need to lay down the sins that beset us. We must ask ourselves: Where are we continually being disobedient? What is blocking our blessing?

The Bible says we are to be blessed beyond measure while our seed is still in the barn, but first, we must open the barn doors and walk out into the sunshine to let the seed be planted. God is asking us to amen Him and obey Him!

Be decisive and determined in taking these steps to getting yourself right with God. He promises to strengthen us and to guide us when we give Him first place in our lives! Let us remember to give God a higher place of honor than our own personal comfort, so that we may be blessed.

There Is Power in Unity

DAY 8

We have all experienced an argument with a family member or close friend, but, even in times when emotions are high, we must remember: A house divided cannot stand.

We must not allow strife in the door! There is a spirit who brings strife, just like there is the spirit of peace, the Holy Spirit. We must not let our guard down and invite in this destructive spirit. When we say hurtful things, and when it is more important for us to be right, we give strife an open door! We invite evil into our home.

The Bible says to give no place to the enemy. This means strife cannot just walk in; it must be invited in. A home filled with strife and division destroys itself.

Mark 3:25 states:

> "SIMILARLY, A FAMILY SPLINTERED BY FEUDING WILL FALL APART."

One disagreement can destroy a relationship. This is an example of strife doing what it does best. It baits you to take offense, but it takes a mature person to overlook this, to know when to say, "No, I'm not going to take this bait. I'm going to stay in peace."

Many times, we think we can change people with our arguments, unfortunately, it only puts them on the defensive, and starts a vicious cycle of discord and division.

The Bible says blessed are the peacemakers; it does not say blessed are those who *think* they are right. You can be so blessed when you stay unified.

Ask God to help you. When you are mature in the Lord, you can have the ability to apologize, even when you know you are right. With Him, you can be the bigger person, and walk away from an argument.

Do not let pride and a haughtiness stop us from receiving blessings. Be a peacemaker!

Run with Endurance

DAY 9

Did you know that we all have an eternal prize for which we are in training? It is the best prize we could ever win: eternity in Heaven with Jesus!

The Bible says we should discipline ourselves like an athlete. 1 Corinthians 9:25-26 states:

"ALL ATHLETES ARE DISCIPLINED IN THEIR TRAINING. THEY DO IT TO WIN A PRIZE THAT WILL FADE AWAY, BUT WE DO IT FOR AN ETERNAL PRIZE. SO, I RUN WITH PURPOSE IN EVERY STEP. I AM NOT JUST SHADOWBOXING."

Do not grow weary in well-doing. We must train to finish God's great commission, fulfilling His will and promises.

Remember, God made us for more than an easy life, and oftentimes, his path for us can be overwhelming. In fact, the apostle Paul consistently reminds us that we must seek God and his word diligently, because difficult times arise and Satan will try to attack. It's easier to persevere through the difficult times because we have the promise of our prize: everlasting life for eternity in Heaven with Jesus. That is an absolute promise from God.

While training, we need to do what God asks of us, and not what our flesh wants to do. We do not want to be disqualified, so we must practice what we preach. We must forget the past, press on to reach the end of the race, and pray for endurance so that we can make it through the tough times, being strengthened in the

Lord. We do not want to get tied up in worldly affairs, repeating the same trek around the mountain.

Lord, help us to run our race with endurance. Help us forget the past and press on to reach our high calling in you!

Holy Discontent

DAY 10

There is a beautiful island near the coast of Honduras, Roatan, that is guarded by a great reef and surrounded by turquoise water. It is called the Little French Key, and I have been blessed to visit this key many times.

Little French Key is also home to a small zoo. The owners of the zoo have rescued injured and neglected animals from all over the world. They created a sanctuary where these animals are greatly cared for and loved.

One of my favorites is a lion named Charlie. Charlie does not know he is a lion: He is as gentle as a house cat and sweet as a puppy. Before the zoo rescued him from his previous life of abuse, he was declawed, and was so scrawny and full of mange that he barely resembled a "king of the jungle." He was nearly dead!

His whole life has been spent in captivity, so he has no idea of the life a wild lion lives. If he was set free now, he would perish. He lived his life defined by the size of his cage.

Like Charlie, how many of us are defined by limitations? The difference is that, as people, we set these limitations for ourselves.

We often feel trapped, like we are missing out on the world. This is what I like to call a holy discontent. Could it be the Holy Spirit prompting you to step out and live your life, on purpose, for Christ?

Ask yourself: What is keeping me confined from living my best life?

The longer we stay in the confinement of the strongholds that hold us back, the more we will become a limited and bound creature of habit. This is where the enemy comes to steal, kill, and destroy.

Decide today to go back and investigate the secret desires of your heart, those seemingly intangible things you shelved long ago. Those very things you cast aside as utter impossibilities can be a reality through Christ. Your best life awaits!

Philippians 4:13 says:

> "For I can do everything through Christ, who gives me strength."

Jesus came to set the captives free. Be determined to step out in faith today!

Answered Prayer

DAY 11

Lately, I have been thinking a lot about the importance of prayer. I believe that God wants us to be bold in our prayers and take authority in Him, through Him, and for Him. This intercession is not about trying to get God to do something; it is about taking our authority, which was bought for us by the precious blood of Jesus Christ.

Yes, Jesus already died for us to have all things in Him! We can never earn salvation; it is a free and unmerited gift. We can only have peace, freedom, divine health, and joy through salvation by coming into an agreement with what the blood has *already* purchased for us.

There is a new way to pray: Simply trust God for what is already yours according to God's Word.

Ephesians 3:20 states:

> "NOW ALL GLORY TO GOD, WHO IS ABLE, THROUGH HIS MIGHTY POWER AT WORK WITHIN US, TO ACCOMPLISH INFINITELY MORE THAN WE MIGHT ASK OR THINK."

We are not beggars, but believers! We must believe to receive, and if we doubt, we will do without. We must stand praising and thanking Jesus that he willingly and painstakingly took care of all our sins, and all our needs. It is the goodness of God that leads men to repentance, not our own works.

Jesus is the only sacrificial lambHe is the Lamb of God that took away our sins and the sins of the world forever! There is no holy protocol or checklist that defines our salvation, or how we get to live our lives in the ultimate flow of blessings. We can merely seek Him first and make Jesus the Lord of our lives.

Trust that He has heard your prayer, knowing that we can have what the Bible says is already ours by just "amen-ing" God and agreeing with His word! Declare it!

Deep Roots

DAY 12

The scripture of Jeremiah 17:8 says:

"They are like trees planted along a riverbank, with roots that reach deep into the water. Such trees are not bothered by the heat or worried by long months of drought. Their leaves stay green, and they never stop producing fruit."

Did you know cedar trees can grow up to 120 feet tall and 30 feet in diameter? They are so powerful and strong. My friends, this is how God sees us, and this is the strength we have in Him. The cedar's root system is twice as deep as the tree is tall. They are rooted deep to withstand anything. Their root systems interlock with roots from other trees, and these trees become immovable, unstoppable, and infallible. It is like linking arms with other strong believers; there is strength and power in numbers.

We, as believers, are to be just as strong and unmoved by our storms of circumstance as the cedar tree. Powerful are we who are deeply rooted in our Lord and Savior, Jesus Christ. We will have strength and longevity, and will flourish abundantly!

Being deeply rooted in Christ means knowing, with absolute certainty, that God is God, and knowing that He can do absolutely anything. Our roots are so strengthened by God's Word that we are immovable and unshakable when the storms come. Deep roots mean that we are not just surface believers, but are protected from the wiles and schemes of the devil.

Because our belief system is far deeper when rooted in the truth, trust God. He will give you strength and peace to withstand any storm. Be flexible, yet strong. When we are deeply rooted in God's Word, we will be able to withstand any storm.

Grow Up in Christ

DAY 13

We are all God's children, and, like all parents, He watches us grow up. God wants us to grow and mature in Him!
Hebrews 6:1 states:

"SO, LET US STOP GOING OVER THE BASIC TEACHINGS ABOUT CHRIST AGAIN AND AGAIN. LET US GO ON INSTEAD AND BECOME MATURE IN OUR UNDERSTANDING. SURELY, WE DON'T NEED TO START AGAIN WITH THE FUNDAMENTAL IMPORTANCE OF REPENTING FROM EVIL DEEDS AND PLACING OUR FAITH IN GOD."

Hebrew 6:3 says:

"AND SO, GOD WILLING, WE WILL MOVE FORWARD TO FURTHER UNDERSTANDING."

For us to grow from infant Christians to mature Christians, we must learn discernment. We must train our senses, our minds, and our bodies to distinguish good from evil. We should pray daily for a greater understanding of all things God. When we read His word, let us ask God to show us mighty things through Him: things that we do not yet know, but that we need to overcome all evil.

While Jesus was here on Earth, He set about doing God's work: He offered prayers, performed great miracles, comforted the hurting, and held a deep reverence for his father. Because of this,

God answered his prayers, and Jesus walked in the supernatural power of His Father.

Life as a Christian is a process. The Bible compares new Christians to babies nursing on milk before graduating to solid food. Too often, we want God's full banquet before we are spiritually and thoroughly capable of digesting it.

As mature Christians, we should be digesting the Word and acting it out, and we should be living examples of His perfect will for us!

The more we know, the more we grow!

Be Made New

DAY 14

Do not be mistaken: God is always guiding us! Our every notion and thought comes from one of two places: the voice of God, or the voice of evil that comes to steal, kill, and destroy.

Always let God's voice trump the voice that says, "It is okay to do my own thing; my sin is not that bad." Do not live in what I like to call "justifiable ignorance."

Like a loving parent, God is never not with us. He is incessantly trying to teach us and lead us. We should be ever mindful to obey and listen to Him, because that is where our peace and victory comes from. When we obey God's Word and refuse to pay attention to what the world is offering, we can walk in the blessings of divine obedience.

Isaiah 48:17-18 reads:

> "This is what the Lord says—your Redeemer, the Holy One of Israel: 'I am the Lord your God, who teaches you what is good for you and leads you along the paths you should follow. Oh, that you had listened to my commands! Then you would have had peace flowing like a gentle river and righteousness rolling over you like waves in the sea.'"

Our unwillingness to pay attention to God's commands invites self-inflicted sorrow and threatens the peace we have through God and God alone! It is like we have stepped out of the covering and divine protection of God through our own free will and willful defiance.

Do not let your heart be hardened by not listening to that small voice. Be free! The Lord has already redeemed His children from slavery to sin through the death of his son, Jesus. When Christ sets us free, we are free indeed. It is time to be made anew; it is time for unspeakable joy as we enter the promised land. God loves you with an everlasting love! Be made new in Him!

Jesus Was Only in a Hurry Once

DAY 15

When Jesus walked the Earth, ministering to others, there was always a sense of calm. He encouraged people to not worry, to stay in peace, and to be at rest.

Even when he had to journey to take care of his sick friend Lazarus, He did not hurry. In fact, He showed up a few days after he had died. He did not hurry when he rose Lazarus from the dead.

His whole ministry portrays Him from a place of peace and rest, except for one time in scripture.

The scripture of Luke 19:5 says:

> "When Jesus came by, He looked up at Zacchaeus and called him by name. 'Zacchaeus!' He said. 'Quick, come down! I must be a guest in your home today.'"

Zacchaeus became a wealthy tax collector by cheating people. He had heard about Jesus' visit and was excited to get a glimpse of him. Zacchaeus climbed up in a tree to see Jesus over the crowds.

But, Jesus knew he was up in the tree; He looked up and called Zacchaeus by his name! We cannot hide from Jesus: He knows us by name, and He always knows exactly where to find us.

Zacchaeus climbed down and accepted Jesus into his home. Jesus wanted him to be saved. He did not wait for Zacchaeus to get cleaned up and get his act together. He did not wait for him to be perfect to be saved. And He did not just stop with Zacchaeus—Jesus saved his entire family! The blessings of the Lord are exponential.

There is no time to waste when it comes to your salvation and your household's salvation. Jesus wants your whole heart now, so what are you waiting for? There is an urgency; call on Jesus' name and be saved!

Faith, Faith and More Faith

DAY 16

Sometimes, we have faith in everyone, except ourselves.

My friends, we must remember, faith is...

... what we cannot see.

... complete trust and confidence in almighty God.

... the opposite of logic.

In all the great stories in the Bible, logic is disproved by great faith.

John 6:5-13 states:

> "Jesus soon saw a huge crowd of people coming to look for Him. Turning to Philip, He asked, 'Where can we buy bread to feed all these people?' He was testing Philip, for he already knew what he was going to do.
>
> Philip replied, 'Even if we worked for months, we wouldn't have enough money to feed them!'
>
> Then Andrew, Simon Peter's brother, spoke up. 'There's a young boy here with five barley loaves and two fish. But what good is that with this huge crowd?'
>
> 'Tell everyone to sit down,' Jesus said. So they all sat down on the grassy slopes. (The men alone numbered about 5,000.) Then Jesus

TOOK THE LOAVES, GAVE THANKS TO GOD, AND DISTRIBUTED THEM TO THE PEOPLE. AFTERWARD HE DID THE SAME WITH THE FISH. AND THEY ALL ATE AS MUCH AS THEY WANTED. AFTER EVERYONE WAS FULL, JESUS TOLD HIS DISCIPLES, 'NOW GATHER THE LEFTOVERS, SO THAT NOTHING IS WASTED.' SO THEY PICKED UP THE PIECES AND FILLED TWELVE BASKETS WITH SCRAPS LEFT BY THE PEOPLE WHO HAD EATEN FROM THE FIVE BARLEY LOAVES."

You see, where there is great faith, there is no room for logic! Faith can move mountains, and it takes over where logic can no longer tread.

Like in this scripture, God first needs believers; He needs true faith. God tells us to amend our ways so that He can do all things. He will take that which seems impossible and make it exceed our needs and surpass understanding.

Believe! God can succeed where logic fails!

Give Us Wisdom Lord

DAY 17

Lately, the Lord has been speaking to me about the importance of wisdom, and it made me think about King Solomon. Of all the things he could have asked for, Solomon asked the Lord for wisdom. And, because of this, God gave it to him liberally, and gave him everything else he needed, including great wealth.

2 Chronicles 1:1-13 says:

> "God said to Solomon, 'Because your greatest desire is to help your people, and you did not ask for wealth, riches, fame, or even the death of your enemies or a long life, but rather you asked for wisdom and knowledge to properly govern my people—I will certainly give you the wisdom and knowledge you requested. But I will also give you wealth, riches, and fame such as no other king has had before you or will ever have in the future!'"

Today, more than ever, we need wisdom to navigate the signs of the times, and to know how to be shrewd and wise in these unprecedented days. God will give us wisdom when we ask Him, and He will give it liberally. And, when we ask, let us ask for divine understanding, so that we can understand the wisdom God gives us and how to put it to good use.

Wisdom from the Lord can be a powerful guide. Each day, we are faced with decisions, many which can be life changing. When we seek God's wisdom, we can make the best choices and the best decisions on God's plan for our lives.

Often, time is wasted when we try to do things on our own, only to meet a dead end or a roadblock ahead. This indecisiveness and lack of wisdom wastes more time, and causes us to have one more trip around the proverbial mountain.

We are not wise in our own site, but, with God, we can have the wisdom of Solomon. Nothing is better than having Godly wisdom!

Seek to Be Transformed

DAY 18

God's Word is the absolute truth and we need to receive it, *not* just read it.

We need to follow the Word and put it into practice, to allow it to transform us, every day, into who God has designed us to be. If we do not put into practice God's Word, and believe in its ability through Jesus to change our lives, then why even read it? What would be the point?

Think of God's Word like an instruction book.

When we buy something that needs to be assembled, there are always instructions included in the box. If we read it and do nothing, then the item remains in pieces, not fully becoming what it was designed to be.

It's the same for us. We must read God's instructions, and allow His Word to put us back together, so that we may be made whole and complete in Jesus! What matters most to God, our Father, is that we completely transform, from the inside-out, into a new creation.

Galatians 6:16 states:

> "MAY GOD'S PEACE AND MERCY BE UPON ALL WHO LIVE BY THIS PRINCIPLE; THEY ARE THE NEW PEOPLE OF GOD."

It is so easy to get caught up in the externals of the world, so we must always be cautious of those who emphasize actions: the religious rules, the endless, rigid lists of "should" and "should not" dos. Living the good life without an inward change will cause us to be shallow and empty in our spiritual walks. Instead, we must walk in the spirit, led by Christ in all we do!

True salvation brings change. We should never want to stay where we are. We must abandon our old lives, die to our flesh, and whole-heartedly seek the Holy Spirit to become more like Christ.

Seek God first, and let His transforming Grace wash away your sins and transform you!

Our Trials Strengthen Us

DAY 19

Our trials and struggles serve a purpose.

There once was a study done concerning a monarch butterfly. As the butterfly was struggling to emerge from its cocoon, the observer felt compassion and decided to help it along. He used an instrument to help cut the butterfly loose from its cocoon, from its struggle. The butterfly emerged so beautiful and brilliant, seeming so effortlessly capable.

But, when the butterfly tried to fly, it could not. It began vigorously flapping its wings. Eventually, it became exhausted and perished. *Why?* It turns out during the struggle to escape the cocoon, a slime is cleansed from a butterfly's wings: a slime that must be removed in order for it to fly. But, because the scientist had helped it emerge from the cocoon, the slime remained weighing down its wings. It could not survive.

Friends, our struggles are good for us.

The scripture of James 1:2-5 says:

> "Dear brothers and sisters, when troubles of any kind come your way, consider it an opportunity for great joy. For you know that when your faith is tested, your endurance has a chance to grow. So let it grow, for when your endurance is fully developed, you will be perfect and complete, needing nothing.

IF YOU NEED WISDOM, ASK OUR GENEROUS GOD, AND HE WILL GIVE IT TO YOU. HE WILL NOT REBUKE YOU FOR ASKING."

Our struggles on their own do not move the hand of God, but they move us to seek Him. These struggles stretch our faith, and then we seek change. Our trials are always beneficial to us, because, through our struggles, we will learn of God's compassion, His mercy, and His grace!

Yes, your trial is temporary, but your struggle is real. Let it make you stronger in the One who holds your future in His victorious palms!

God Wants to Use You

DAY 20

Are you ready for God to use you for His good work?

This is the question we must ask ourselves. Of course, none of us are ever perfect, but we must continually strive to be ready for anything God has in store for us. How do we do that? We must start with a self-check of the condition of our hearts.

While imprisoned, Paul writes to Timothy, whom he regarded as a son. In his last letter to Timothy, he tells him to be strong, and reminds him that God did not give us a spirit of fear, but one of power, love, and self-discipline, and tells him to remain "pure".

In 2 Timothy 2:19-21, Paul's letter says:

> "But God's truth stands firm like a foundation stone with this inscription: 'The Lord knows those who are His,' and 'All who belong to the Lord must turn away from evil.'
>
> In a wealthy home some utensils are made of gold and silver, and some are made of wood and clay. The expensive utensils are used for special occasions, and the cheap ones are for everyday use. If you keep yourself pure, you will be a special utensil for honorable use. Your life will be clean, and you will be ready for the Master to use you for every good work."

What grabs my heart is the description of utensils. Most of us have "everyday" dishes and utensils. When we use them, we do not worry much if they eventually become scratched or cracked, because they are not especially valuable to us. But, the silver and the china are only brought out for special occasions, and handled with extreme care.

Paul is saying, if we keep ourselves pure, we will always be like the silver; we can always be a special utensil, ready for God to use us for His every good work.

We must stay pure and remain close to God, so we can ask Him to reveal to us what He wants to do with our lives. We must be the kind of person that Christ can use for His divine purposes here on Earth!

Stay Prayed Up

DAY 21

To be strong, an army must prepare in every conceivable way to stay protected. They must utilize heavy armor, be fully instructed on how to use their weaponry, and be alert for sightings of the enemy. They learn defensive and offensive strategies in order to prevent casualties.

Friends, our spiritual battles need to be handled in very much the same way! Though our battles are supernatural, we still need to be completely strategic in our battle plan.

Every day, I pray out loud Psalm 91 for protection over myself, my family, my friends, my ministry, and for this nation. I break it down, line by line, and physically see myself protected, covered, as I declare these words over every concern I have and every situation.

Psalm 91:1-5 states:

> "Those who live in the shelter of the Most High will find rest in the shadow of the Almighty. This I declare about the Lord: He alone is my refuge, my place of safety; He is my God, and I trust Him. For He will rescue you from every trap and protect you from deadly disease.

> HE WILL COVER YOU WITH HIS FEATHERS.
> HE WILL SHELTER YOU WITH HIS WINGS.
> HIS FAITHFUL PROMISES ARE YOUR ARMOR AND
> PROTECTION. DO NOT BE AFRAID OF THE TERRORS OF
> THE NIGHT, NOR THE ARROW THAT FLIES IN THE DAY."

We must physically see ourselves putting on the whole armor of God, and have our swords and shields ready for battle, ready to overcome. We must be prepared with an arsenal of God's Word. We need to realize and know who we are in Christ—we are sword-bearers of the Word.

Psalm 91:9-11 continues:

> "IF YOU MAKE THE LORD YOUR REFUGE,
> IF YOU MAKE THE MOST HIGH YOUR SHELTER,
> NO EVIL WILL CONQUER YOU; NO PLAGUE WILL
> COME NEAR YOUR HOME. FOR HE WILL ORDER
> HIS ANGELS TO PROTECT YOU WHEREVER YOU GO."

Stay prayed up to be protected! Be a warrior of the Word!

Made Whole in Him

DAY 22

The brilliant, steadfast word of God is so alive and unchanging that it has the power to transform any and every life.

Psalm 107:20 reads:

> "HE SENT OUT HIS WORD AND HEALED THEM, SNATCHING THEM FROM THE DOOR OF DEATH."

There is executive power in the Word of God. When we speak it, it acts as an unrelenting sword, piercing through any evil and bringing miraculous change.

In the Bible, Jesus heals the man at the pool of Bethesda (John 5:1-5). I often get asked why Jesus only healed this one man at the pool, and not the other disease-ridden people.

The answer is because these people were doubtful; they could not see beyond what they had placed their hope in. Many just kept their eyes on the pool: their faith was in the waters. They had no eyes for Jesus!

God's Word is unchanging. When spoken and declared, its supernatural power still brings forth creative miracles today! The power of God's Word has not been diminished or changed throughout the centuries.

But, how many of us are overlooking the miracle that is in Jesus? How many of us are overlooking He who is right here with us? Jesus is waiting on you to invite Him into your life, to bring transformation, healing, deliverance, and restoration.

When we pray, our hope should not be in our prayers, but in the One who is able to answer them. Many of us keep our trust and hope in the things we can see with our eyes—the things we deem provable—but, faith is always in what we cannot see. We need to set our eyes on God, instead of on things.

It is God's will for you to be whole in every area of your life. Jesus asks, "Wilt thou be made whole?" Give Him your answer!

God's Word Has Staying Power

DAY 23

Good or bad, true or untrue, our words and declarations over our lives have *stinging* power. Often, we believe these lies, and we begin to take on the meaning of these negative words, including negative words we have declared about ourselves.

On the other hand, God's words have *staying* power. His words are lasting and true, and will overcome any negativity that has ever been spoken over us. Yet, how many of us believe what the enemy is speaking over what the word of God says about our lives?

Stinging power, or staying power!

Psalm 46:1-3 Says:

> "GOD IS OUR REFUGE AND STRENGTH,
> ALWAYS READY TO HELP IN TIMES OF TROUBLE.
> SO, WE WILL NOT FEAR WHEN EARTHQUAKES COME
> AND THE MOUNTAINS CRUMBLE INTO THE SEA.
> LET THE OCEANS ROAR AND FOAM. LET THE
> MOUNTAINS TREMBLE AS THE WATERS SURGE!"

God calls you what you are before it happens. People will call you what you are after it happens. We see this in the scripture.

God called Abraham the "father of nations" long before it was true. It made no sense that Abraham and Sarah, an elderly couple well past their child-bearing years, would ever see God's Words come to pass. How would he have one child, let alone become the father of nations? Yet, God spoke it, so it happened!

David was called to be a future king while he was a mere teenager, a shepherd boy. David was not even in the lineup of Jesse's sons; his own father did not call him into the house for a chance at consideration. And yet, God knew exactly where he was, and no one could stop what God had ordained for David. God supernaturally qualified David because he had a heart for God.

God knows where you are, who has left you out of the lineup, and who has deemed you unworthy! What He says about you is the truth for your life, and there is a plan for your life that no one can steal, unless you believe the lies the enemy has laid before you.

It is time to abandon every "you will never amount to anything," and every "you're not qualified enough, smart enough, good enough, pretty enough, talented enough…" Lies! Bury those lies in the sea of forgetfulness, and cast them away through your authority in Jesus

Like Abraham, David, Joseph, and many others, start declaring what God has said, no matter how impossible it seems! God can do what men can not.

No More Delays

DAY 24

My friends, if you have been praying for something, but feel like your prayers have not been answered, it is time to start praying against delay. It is time to ask God to send angels to bind and hold back the spirit of delay, so that your prayers can be answered.

Daniel 10:12-14 states:

> "Then he said, 'Don't be afraid, Daniel. Since the first day you began to pray for understanding and to humble yourself before your God, your request has been heard in Heaven. I have come in answer to your prayer. But for twenty-one days the spirit prince of the kingdom of Persia blocked my way. Then Michael, one of the archangels, came to help me, and I left him there with the spirit prince of the kingdom of Persia. Now I am here to explain what will happen to your people in the future, for this vision concerns a time yet to come.'"

Isn't the revelation in this scripture amazing? It says that Daniel's prayers were heard, but the spirit prince (delay) was hindering his breakthrough. But, then Archangel Michael was sent to bind that spirit, so that Daniel could receive his breakthrough once and for all!

I feel God is revealing new evidence to us about how to pray. God is faithful to his promises, so He always tells us what we need to know to receive our victory.

My friends, what is delaying your breakthrough? Is something holding you back: a destiny-robber, a delayer of promises, a hindering spirit? Let us pray the name of Jesus that our lives will move forward, with no more delays or limitations, and that we will rule and reign in life over the spirit of delay. We decree our victories to come forth! No more hindrances or delays!

The Meaning Of Mountains

DAY 25

The scripture of Psalm 3:4 says:

> "I CRIED OUT TO THE LORD, AND HE ANSWERED ME FROM HIS HOLY MOUNTAIN."

While reading about the transfiguration of Jesus, on the mountain, in the Gospel of Mark, I realized something about the importance of mountains, and had a revelation from the Lord: in the Bible, mountains symbolize two vastly different things.

On one hand, I noticed a mountain is often associated with closeness to God. It symbolizes a readiness to receive His words. God appeared to Moses and Elijah on mountains, and Jesus often took the disciples to Mount Hermon or Mount Tabor. It is on the mountaintop, high and lifted, where we are close to God and can hear Him clearly.

The Scripture talks about how mountains can be a symbol for trials. The Scripture shows us that it is possible, through faith, prayer, and declaration, to make mountains into level plains in our lives.

Mark 11:23 states:

> "I TELL YOU THE TRUTH, YOU CAN SAY TO THIS MOUNTAIN, 'MAY YOU BE LIFTED UP AND THROWN INTO THE SEA,' AND IT WILL HAPPEN. BUT YOU MUST REALLY BELIEVE IT WILL HAPPEN AND HAVE NO DOUBT IN YOUR HEART."

God brings us through our mountains (trials), which we need to level; this is also where we are drawn so incredibly close to God and can see His hand revealed.

Never be afraid to confront evil (your mountains of adversity), and to take your authority in Jesus onto the mountaintop! Jesus will always go with us and meet us on those mountaintops. We do not have to search for Jesus like the disciples did.

Let us be ready and willing for Jesus to lead us to the mountaintop, and to receive great revelations of the mysteries of His divine will.

Follow Peace

DAY 26

When we are right with God, we will 'KNOW' peace. When we are off-track, there is 'NO' peace.

Isaiah 48:17 reads:

"THIS IS WHAT THE LORD SAYS—YOUR REDEEMER, THE HOLY ONE OF ISRAEL: 'I AM THE LORD YOUR GOD, WHO TEACHES YOU WHAT IS GOOD FOR YOU AND LEADS YOU ALONG THE PATHS YOU SHOULD FOLLOW. OH, THAT YOU HAD LISTENED TO MY COMMANDS! THEN YOU WOULD HAVE HAD PEACE FLOWING LIKE A GENTLE RIVER AND RIGHTEOUSNESS ROLLING OVER YOU LIKE WAVES IN THE SEA.'"

God is always guiding us, and His way will always be right, even when we are kicking against it and our flesh wants us to go in the exact opposite direction. When that small voice (the Holy Spirit) starts to gently convict you, then you are off track! He is, and always will be, our voice of reason.

Isaiah 48:22 states:

"'But there is no peace for the wicked,' says the Lord."

We need to listen to the Lord's Word! The flesh can come up with many reasons to justify disobedience. The enemy knows the Word, and can twist God's words to fit our agendas. We must be so steadfast in our walk with Jesus that we are immovable, so that we can immediately recognize the carrot of the enemy being dangled in front of us.

We must stay strong and follow peace. God will make our way plain and simple, and He always confirms his plan. We can make our plans, but He is the one who orders our every step. Spend time with the Lord, and He will make the crooked places straight.

God is our loving Father, and He is never not with us; He is always trying to teach us and lead us. When we obey the Word, and refuse to pay attention to what the world is offering, we can walk in the blessings of divine obedience, and know His sweetest and purest peace.

God is an Overflow God

DAY 27

When God restores, He multiplies.
2 Kings 4:3-6 states:

"And Elisha said, 'Borrow as many empty jars as you can from your friends and neighbors. Then go into your house with your sons and shut the door behind you. Pour olive oil from your flask into the jars, setting each one aside when it is filled.'

So she did as she was told. Her sons kept bringing jars to her, and she filled one after another. Soon every container was full to the brim!

'Bring me another jar,' she said to one of her sons.

'There aren't any more!' he told her. And then the olive oil stopped flowing."

In this passage, it is evident to see how God is the God of overflow, of providing more than enough. Here, Elisha helps a poor widow whose husband had served Elisha. After he passed away, creditors came to the woman's house, threatening to take away her sons as slaves for the debt owed by her husband.

What is interesting is that Elisha said to the widow, "What do you have in the house?" The widow only had a small flask of olive oil. I am sure she was thinking, 'How it is possible that this tiny flask of oil does not run out?"

But, she was obedient in her faith, which allowed her to receive a miracle. She did what she was told, and every jar her sons brought her was filled to the brim!

God could have just miraculously filled the jars and required nothing on her part, but God does require obedience on our part—we need to have faith. She, and her sons, were there and able to witness the goodness of the overflowing, miraculous love of God. They were partakers of a miracle of God's love and provision.

You see, God uses what we have, and His abundance only stops flowing when we have no more capacity to contain it! Let God use your faith and obedience to bring forth your miracle.

Is Your Heart Hardened?

DAY 28

The scripture in Proverbs 4:23 says:

> "GUARD YOUR HEART ABOVE ALL ELSE, FOR IT DETERMINES THE COURSE OF YOUR LIFE."

Above all else, God wants us to guard our hearts. But, why is this so important?

It is important because all things pertaining to life flow from our hearts. The Bible says that, out of the abundance of the heart, the mouth speaks. So many times, we can hear one's hurt flowing through the negativity of their mindset and attitude; they are constantly faultfinding and complaining about everything.

This negativity can create a hardened heart towards the Lord, and like a callus, our hearts become so hardened that we no longer allow the good stuff in, and the bad stuff gets trapped inside, as well.

A hardened heart is a disease that needs to be addressed and healed.

Our hearts are the soil for the seeds that God wants to plant. He wants to give us seeds of hope and victory. But, many times, our hearts are so filled with pride, jealousy, bitterness, and anger that it prevents us from turning to God.

Our hearts are the source for the springs of all life, so should we not place the most protective armor and guards around it? How do we protect ourselves?

Recognize the enemy's plots and refuse to let them be planted. Replace the wrong thoughts with the right thoughts, according to

God's Word. Do not allow seeds of discouragement, bitterness, and anger to affect your faith.

Allow God to wash you clean, and allow the healing power of the blood of Jesus to cleanse and pluck out all the bitter roots that have callused your heart. Repent, forgive, and let your heart be softened by the love of Jesus! From the abundance of the heart, the mouth speaks!

Draw Near to God

DAY 29

Today, I want to focus on the name of the place called Goshen. In Hebrew, Goshen means "drawing near." I knew, in my spirit, that God wanted me to study this further.

Goshen is referred to in the Bible many times. In the scripture of Exodus, God says that Goshen is where His people live. Yes, Goshen is where we, God's people, live and draw near to God.

Goshen is also mentioned in Genesis 45:10-11. The Scripture says:

> "'You can live in the region of Goshen, where you can be near me with all your children and grandchildren, your flocks and herds, and everything you own. I will take care of you there, for there are still five years of famine ahead of us. Otherwise you, your household, and all your animals will starve.'"

He sent His people to Goshen for safety, rest, renewal, and protection. When we are drawing near to God, we are also kept secure in His protection and in His care. We must seek Him first, as it is a two-way street: The Bible says when we draw near to God, He draws near to us.

The second half of that scripture tells of trials looming up ahead. It says there will still be famines and trouble, but it also tells God's people to worry not, because they will be in Goshen. We must remember this in our times of trial.

God desires intimacy with us, not only because He loves us, but because He knows that, through that intimacy with Him, we will be in that secret place of protection. Here, He can keep us safe from the enemy, and provide for us our every need.

Goshen, drawing near, is where we will trust God to reveal to us the great mysteries of His will. It is where our own plans can be replaced with God's plans, as He directs our every step. We can go to the land of Goshen by drawing near to God!

It Is Time to Flourish

DAY 30

In my spirit, I heard God say many of His people are not thriving, and that we are not all flourishing.

What does it mean to flourish? It means to prosper, to grow, and to thrive.

Psalm 92:12 says:

"BUT THE GODLY WILL FLOURISH LIKE PALM TREES AND GROW STRONG LIKE THE CEDARS OF LEBANON."

You see, God wants all things to work together for our good. He wants us to be victorious in every area of our lives. The above scripture references palm trees, which do not snap and break during storms. They are extraordinarily strong, and can bend and sway. They are easily adaptable, and can withstand the harsh winds and storms.

Through God, we can be like these palm trees.

Know that we get to choose whether our imaginations and thoughts are positive or negative. Be warned, however, that these thoughts will eventually become a self-fulfilling prophecy. Therefore, we should not allow our imaginations to see ourselves as poor, sick, tired, or depressed. If we quit and give up, our imaginations will be negative, and we will have no more hope.

Instead, take God's Word, and let it help you flourish and thrive. Say things that are not as they are, speak life into your situations, and live with expectancy. When we have positive expectations and hope, we will flourish! We will bend and not break.

Through God, we can bend, adapt, and adjust in times of adversity. We can thrive, no matter what is going on around us, if God is the One in whom we put our trust!

It is time to start believing that the Lord wants us to flourish in every area of our lives. We can get our hope back by encouraging ourselves in His Word, and by speaking positively in every area of our lives.

Jesus, Do You Know Him?

DAY 31

One morning, while reading the Word, I realized how much God wants us to utterly understand that Jesus Christ has already paid the debt for our sins. Christ is the complete fullness of God, and when we learn what Christ is like, when we know Him, we see what we need to become.

Paul spoke about the importance of knowing Jesus and his teachings.

Colossians 1:9-10 states:

> "SO WE HAVE NOT STOPPED PRAYING FOR YOU SINCE WE FIRST HEARD ABOUT YOU. WE ASK GOD TO GIVE YOU COMPLETE KNOWLEDGE OF HIS WILL AND TO GIVE YOU SPIRITUAL WISDOM AND UNDERSTANDING. THEN THE WAY YOU LIVE WILL ALWAYS HONOR AND PLEASE THE LORD, AND YOUR LIVES WILL PRODUCE EVERY KIND OF GOOD FRUIT. ALL THE WHILE, YOU WILL GROW AS YOU LEARN TO KNOW GOD BETTER AND BETTER."

Paul wanted us to know that even though we must be able to understand what the Word means for us to be able to apply it, this knowledge is empty if we do not have a close personal relationship with Jesus. It is only through Salvation, by His bloodshed and resurrection, for the forgiveness of sin, that we were transferred out of the darkness and into the light. Now, we must desire a personal relationship with Christ like never before.

There are many people who can quote scripture, and know the words of the Bible cover to cover, yet they have no fruit in their lives. They are like empty vessels: They have head knowledge, but no heart knowledge.

The knowledge of God is available to all of us, not just a select few. It is open to everyone who desires and longs to learn more about God, and to those who diligently seek intimacy with Him.

We must seek God's understanding of how to apply His Word to our lives, and do so daily for guidance and wisdom, as we allow the Holy Spirit to gain access to our innermost being. Only then we will know Jesus and His perfect love for us.

Life Is a Collaboration with God

DAY 32

We were never meant to go at life alone. Life is meant to be a collaboration with God!

In the Bible, we often see God's collaboration in the lives of His people. God would often lead His people to take action, while masking the big picture.

Many times, God does not want us to know the whole story. Why? If we did, it might be too much for us to handle; we would see the impossibilities of what God is asking us to do. But, God is calling us to simply trust Him!

Romans 4:16-17 says:

"SO THE PROMISE IS RECEIVED BY FAITH. IT IS GIVEN AS A FREE GIFT. AND WE ARE ALL CERTAIN TO RECEIVE IT, WHETHER OR NOT WE LIVE ACCORDING TO THE LAW OF MOSES, IF WE HAVE FAITH LIKE ABRAHAM'S. FOR ABRAHAM IS THE FATHER OF ALL WHO BELIEVE. THAT IS WHAT THE SCRIPTURES MEAN WHEN GOD TOLD HIM, 'I HAVE MADE YOU THE FATHER OF MANY NATIONS.' THIS HAPPENED BECAUSE ABRAHAM BELIEVED IN THE GOD WHO BRINGS THE DEAD BACK TO LIFE AND WHO CREATES NEW THINGS OUT OF NOTHING."

Abraham never wavered, he believed in God's promise. In fact, it made his faith grow stronger. Abraham's life was marked by mistakes, sins, and failures, but he consistently trusted God. If he had only looked upon his own resources, he would have been faced with impossibilities and complete despair. But, Abraham looked to God, and waited for Him to fulfill His Word, His brilliant promise.

Friends, it is time for us to take the leap into a new, deeper level of faith in God. We can learn to navigate gray in a black-and-white world. We do not have to hold the entire blueprint in our hand, but we must step out together with our Lord, and know He will never forsake us.

We have all we need. Grab ahold of God's hand and fly!

Do You Have Doubts?

DAY 33

Friends, let me ask you: Do you have doubts? Has your faith ever been shaken?

If so, you are not alone.

In Matthew 11:11, Jesus says:

> "I TELL YOU THE TRUTH, OF ALL WHO HAVE EVER LIVED, NONE IS GREATER THAN JOHN THE BAPTIST. YET EVEN THE LEAST PERSON IN THE KINGDOM OF HEAVEN IS GREATER THAN HE IS!"

Jesus describes John as the greatest man that ever lived. And yet, while in prison, John *himself* had doubts that Jesus was the messiah.

Since his birth, it was understood that John would be set apart for the service of God, and he never wavered in being faithful to the call. When John baptized Jesus, he heard an audible voice from the Father, saying that this was His son, in whom he was well pleased. He witnessed the dove as a representation of the Holy Spirit.

He knew Jesus. He loved Jesus. He witnessed the miracles of Jesus. And yet...

Doubts came!

We all can have doubts, from time to time. When our faith has been shaken, when trauma and turmoil rock our world, it can cause us to cry out and ask, "Is any of this real? God, are you really there for me?"

My friends, we all have a calling. We all have something we were born to do, and a purpose in Christ.

In the times of uncertainty that cause our knees to buckle, we often take our eyes off Jesus and put them on our own circumstances. This is where the enemy would love to cause doubt and lead us away from our call. But, nothing can stop what God has ordained for your life.

Be obedient to the Word, and trust your purpose over doubts. Keep your eyes on Jesus!

God Listens

DAY 34

King Solomon, son of King David, was an extremely wise man, and, like his father, praised the Lord continuously. Because of his wisdom, it serves us well to pray in the same manner as he did.

In 1 Kings 8:56-61, King Solomon's prayer is as follows:

"Praise the Lord who has given rest to his people Israel, just as he promised. Not one word has failed of all the wonderful promises he gave through his servant Moses.
May the Lord our God be with us as he was with our ancestors; may he never leave us or abandon us. May he give us the desire to do his will in everything and to obey all the commands, decrees, and regulations that he gave our ancestors.

And may these words that I have prayed in the presence of the Lord be before him constantly, day and night, so that the Lord our God may give justice to me and to his people Israel, according to each day's needs. Then people all over the earth will know that the Lord alone is God and there is no other. And may you be completely faithful to the Lord our God. May you always obey his decrees and commands, just as you are doing today.'"

In his powerful prayer from the scripture above, King Solomon made five basic requests in his prayer, and we can use the outline of these requests as a pattern when we pray over ourselves and our families, and over every other need we have.

When he prayed, Solomon asked for the presence of God to be with him, the desire to always do God's will, and the strength to obey his commands. He asked for God to supply his needs, and for the world to know God.

Solomon's prayer habits are a great example for us to follow. When we ask for God's Will for our lives, we are simultaneously canceling out our own plans. We avoid our fleshly desires, which could lead us down a destructive path that causes us to live according to the world's standards and not God's. God knows that we are not infallible against the exploits of the devil, but He also knows if our true desire is to please Him or ourselves. God hears us; He listens to our silent pleas and desires.

May God's will always trump our own will!

Make Room for Jesus

DAY 35

What are we making room for in our lives, and what are we just letting pass us by?

The Bible says it is the small foxes that spoil the vine. In other words, we can get so distracted by all the little, monotonous things, and become so inundated with the *seemingly* important things, that we are not making room for the *truly* important things.

These humdrum, little time-stealers are all the things that keep our eyes off Jesus, and keep us overwhelmed and living in sheer frustration. We, as a solo act of one, are trying to keep all the balls in the air, but, our endless efforts are futile without God.

John 15:5 states:

"'YES, I AM THE VINE; YOU ARE THE BRANCHES. THOSE WHO REMAIN IN ME, AND I IN THEM, WILL PRODUCE MUCH FRUIT. FOR, APART FROM ME, YOU CAN DO NOTHING.'"

You + Jesus = a majority. He is the vine that allows us to thrive. We need Jesus!

The day-to-day juggling act that causes us to drag ourselves to bed at night, declaring, in complete exhaustion, that we have made it through another day, is not of God! No. Life was never meant to be this way. We are supposed to have and enjoy our everyday life, and live, and move, and *have* our being in Christ.

How do we do that? We need to make room for God first! Seek Him first!

If we do not make room in our hearts, if we are too busy or distracted by what is on the TV, our computer screens, or other worldly things, we will not be able to hear from God. Without Him, we can be easily overcome by the world's enticements, which leads to sin and destruction.

I think it is time we make room in our hearts. Let us be the empty vessels, washed clean and ready, so that we do not miss out on all that God has in store for us.

Keep Your Eyes on Jesus

DAY 36

When we keep our eyes on Jesus, we can do amazing things. But, when we take our eyes off Jesus, it is a completely different story.

When Jesus walked on water, his disciples were in absolute awe. In Peter's exuberance, his confidence soared, and he boldly asked Jesus if he too could walk on water. Without hesitation, Jesus invited him out of the safety of the boat and into the waves.

Matthew 14:28-30 states:

> "THEN PETER CALLED TO HIM, 'LORD, IF IT'S REALLY YOU, TELL ME TO COME TO YOU, WALKING ON THE WATER.'
>
> 'YES, COME,' JESUS SAID.
>
> SO PETER WENT OVER THE SIDE OF THE BOAT AND WALKED ON THE WATER TOWARD JESUS. BUT WHEN HE SAW THE STRONG WIND AND THE WAVES, HE WAS TERRIFIED AND BEGAN TO SINK. 'SAVE ME, LORD!' HE SHOUTED."

Through Jesus, Peter was able to walk on water! But, when he took his eyes off Jesus, and instead turned them towards the waves, he began to sink.

I love this story because there is such a picture of the love and faithfulness of Jesus packed into a few short scriptures.

First, we learn that we must keep our eyes on Jesus and not on the waves, or any of the other chaos and circumstances that inundate us in this life. When looking to Jesus, we must practice tunnel vision.

Second, even though Peter failed to stay focused on Jesus, the very second that he said, "Lord, save me!" Jesus did not hesitate for a second. We know that, even when we are off-course, Jesus will be right there, ready and willing to save us. He loves us too much to let us fall.

We must keep our eyes on Jesus! Let us keep our eyes laser-focused on our wonderful Lord and Savior, so that we can do all things through Him who strengthens us!

God Has Already Done It

DAY 37

Before we ever lived a day on Earth, God had gone before us and anticipated our every need.

Ephesians 2:8 states:

> "GOD SAVED YOU BY HIS GRACE WHEN YOU BELIEVED. AND YOU CAN'T TAKE CREDIT FOR THIS; IT IS A GIFT FROM GOD."

Yes, He did this through His Grace: He knew how many people would populate the earth, He knew how much air we would need, He prepared the food supply, the animals, trees, and water, and planned ahead for our shelter. He even gave humans and animals the ability to procreate, and gave plants seeds to replenish themselves.

God leaves no stone left unturned when supplying for our needs. He has done this long before we ever were born! In fact, God did not make man until the fifth day. He made everything else, anticipating that he would create man. We were never an afterthought.

We were the reason for everything else!

God's anticipation of our every need still holds true today. He just did not stop that day. No, He did something even greater: He sent His Son to save us!

Jesus paid the price for everything in advance of our needs. God once again anticipated and provided us with a way to spend eternity with Him. Jesus died so that we could have salvation, divine health, and provision in every area of our lives.

He has provided everything we need by His amazing grace, but we need to activate our faith to appropriate God's grace. Faith is ultimately just a positive response on our part to what God has already done for us by His grace. We cannot ever say that we have been saved by faith, or by grace alone: We must put the two together!

Gratitude and Faith

DAY 38

If we are to live like Jesus, we must study what Jesus did while he was on Earth.

1 John 4:17 says:

> "And as we live in God, our love grows more perfect. So we will not be afraid on the day of judgment, but we can face Him with confidence because we live like Jesus here in this world."

While there is so much to learn, we must know we can ask for wisdom and great understanding, because the Bible says God will give it to us liberally.

The story of Jesus healing ten men with leprosy shows what a tiny mustard seed of faith can do. Because, at the time, leprosy was a highly contagious and deadly disease, those infected were required to stay far away from others. In those days, a priest would have to declare people disease-free before they could return to society.

In Luke 17:14, we see what Jesus said to the lepers:

> "He looked at them and said, 'Go show yourselves to the priests.' And as they went, they were cleansed of their leprosy."

The lepers were sent by Jesus to a priest *before* they were healed. The men responded in faith, and then Jesus healed them while they were on their way!

Yet, in the second half of this scripture, only *one* of those men returned to Jesus to praise Him and thank Him. A mustard seed of faith and an attitude of gratitude are an important combination!

The scripture shows that it is entirely possible to receive God's great gifts with an ungrateful spirit, but, there is so much more for the grateful man that returned. He was to learn that his faith played an important role in his healing, and he was able to share his joy with Jesus in fellowship, praise, and love.

Our trust in God must be so strong that we act on what God says in His word even before we see any evidence that it will ever work. By living with an attitude of gratitude, no matter what we are facing, we gain an appreciation for God's goodness and faithfulness.

Behold! All Things Are Possible!

DAY 39

In the Gospel of Mark, we learn that Jesus healed a paralyzed man. The paralyzed man's friends carried him over to the house where Jesus was speaking. The house was so packed with visitors that there was no more room left. It seemed impossible for the men to get close enough to Jesus.

But, when we are hungry and thirsty for the power and presence of the Lord, nothing can stop us from being amid God's supernatural plan!

These men recognized the great need of their friend, and were moved with compassion to spring into action. Being so determined in their faith, they dug a hole through the roof above Jesus' head. They lowered the man through the hole, to get him to Jesus.

The Bible says that, when Jesus saw the man's face, He said to the paralyzed man, "My child, your sins are forgiven." Then, Jesus turned to the paralyzed man and told him to stand up and go home.

Mark 2:12 says:

> "AND THE MAN JUMPED UP, GRABBED HIS MAT, AND WALKED OUT THROUGH THE STUNNED ONLOOKERS. THEY WERE ALL AMAZED AND PRAISED GOD, EXCLAIMING, 'WE'VE NEVER SEEN ANYTHING LIKE THIS BEFORE!'"

The phrase "We've never seen anything like this before" stirs my heart! I believe life should be naturally supernatural. If there is anything that God is dissatisfied with, it is our unbelief. He is dissatisfied when we put Him in a box and fail to believe in the miraculous, and when we fail to believe that God is still on the throne. God has never stopped being God!

How many times are we stopping just short of our miracle because of what we have deemed to be impossible? God can make a way when there seems to be no way; that is how and when He gets all the glory!

May we continuously seek His presence, and pass the threshold of impossibilities to get to that place in our hearts where God meets us. All things are possible in Christ!

Are You Missing God?

DAY 40

We all go through times in our lives when we feel like we are absolutely alone on this planet. We feel like no one understands what we are going through, and we let our fears contaminate our faith.

But, even when you feel all alone, God has never left you.

While reading the story of Elijah in 1 Kings, we learn that Elijah thought he was the only person left who was still true to God. He witnessed both the king's court and the priesthood become entirely corrupt, and he felt alone. After running for his life from the enemy at Mount Carmel, he was discouraged. His fear clouded his judgement, and he could not hear God.

Often, we are so tempted to think that we are the only ones remaining faithful to a task, and we are left feeling all alone. However, self-pity is a bait of Satan, and it will dilute our faith.

When we are tempted to feel like all the burdens are on our shoulders, we must remember what Jesus said in Matthew 11:28-30:

> "THEN JESUS SAID, 'COME TO ME, ALL OF YOU WHO ARE WEARY AND CARRY HEAVY BURDENS, AND I WILL GIVE YOU REST. TAKE MY YOKE UPON YOU. LET ME TEACH YOU, BECAUSE I AM HUMBLE AND GENTLE AT HEART, AND YOU WILL FIND REST FOR YOUR SOULS. FOR MY YOKE IS EASY TO BEAR, AND THE BURDEN I GIVE YOU IS LIGHT.'"

Rest assured, even if we do not see it, God sends us help to strengthen our faith, so we can obey and stay the course. God even sends help even when we feel hopeless. God is our advocate. The minute we pray, God hears us!

Is God trying to get your attention? Your answer may just come in a quiet whisper when spending alone time with our Lord. Cast your cares; God is whispering!

Pleasing the Lord

DAY 41

While reading the following scripture in Colossians recently, I thought about what it means to please the Lord.

Colossians 1:9-10 states:

> "SO WE HAVE NOT STOPPED PRAYING FOR YOU SINCE WE FIRST HEARD ABOUT YOU. WE ASK GOD TO GIVE YOU COMPLETE KNOWLEDGE OF HIS WILL AND TO GIVE YOU SPIRITUAL WISDOM AND UNDERSTANDING. THEN THE WAY YOU LIVE WILL ALWAYS HONOR AND PLEASE THE LORD, AND YOUR LIVES WILL PRODUCE EVERY KIND OF GOOD FRUIT. ALL THE WHILE, YOU WILL GROW AS YOU LEARN TO KNOW GOD BETTER AND BETTER."

Are we walking in a way that is bearing good fruit, and pleasing God? We all must ask ourselves if we are truly walking in a manner worthy of the Lord.

I think this question is something we should ask ourselves routinely. We should all do a heart check-up and make sure that we are on the right path, and that we have not strayed through a hardness of heart from gossip, anger, bitterness, greed, insecurity, hurts, and unforgiveness. We must ask God to show us any place where we may have gotten off track, and then we must repent and ask for forgiveness.

Let us ask God to help us bear good fruit, and to increase our knowledge of the things He has in store for us, and the things that He would have us do. We are all here for such a time as this. Let us make the most of this time, and walk in a manner that is worthy of the Lord and pleases Him mightily!

Peace and Fullness in Christ

DAY 42

As Jesus was, so are we to be. In Jesus, there is a place of shelter, rest, peace, and faith. There is nothing else like it.

We, as Christians, must press in to receive all that we have available to us through the blood of Jesus. There is an excellence of Christ that can never be completely understood by the human mind: We cannot fathom a love so vast, immense, unconditional, and perfect. It is through the Holy Spirit that we can ask for an understanding and wisdom to learn the depths of Christ.

Philippians 3:9 says:

> "AND BECOME ONE WITH HIM. I NO LONGER COUNT ON MY OWN RIGHTEOUSNESS THROUGH OBEYING THE LAW; RATHER, I BECOME RIGHTEOUS THROUGH FAITH IN CHRIST. FOR GOD'S WAY OF MAKING US RIGHT WITH HIMSELF DEPENDS ON FAITH."

We must not strive for our own desires or plans, but rest in the perfect plan of God, and be settled in our hearts that, in Him, there is nothing we shall want; there is no lack, disease, or fear. In Christ, it is impossible for a child of God to fail!

The Scriptures declare unto us that we, as believers, are to be like him. What can move us from the place of omnipotent power? Shall tribulation, or persecution, or peril, or sword? No! Shall life, or death, or principalities, or powers? No! We are more than conquerors through him that loves us. And, through this knowledge, we can have perfect peace that is only found in him! We are immovable in Christ!

There is such a transformation, a regeneration, by the power of the Holy Spirit of the living God, that makes us see that there is a place to win in Jesus, so that we may stand completely made whole in Him. Perfect peace is found only in Him!

A Road in the Desert

DAY 43

God always makes a way.
   Isaiah 43:18-19 says:

> "BUT FORGET ALL THAT—IT IS NOTHING COMPARED TO WHAT I AM GOING TO DO. FOR I AM ABOUT TO DO SOMETHING NEW. SEE, I HAVE ALREADY BEGUN! DO YOU NOT SEE IT? I WILL MAKE A PATHWAY THROUGH THE WILDERNESS. I WILL CREATE RIVERS IN THE DRY WASTELAND."

   What does God mean when He says He is making roads through the wilderness?

   In my time with the Lord, I feel like He has shown me that the wilderness is an extremely vast and open wasteland, it has no roads, no landmarks, and no points to help us find our way. But, God always makes a way!

   When God makes a road through the wilderness, He is giving us a path to follow. He is giving us a way out of desolation; He gives us a road that leads us out of our aimless meandering, one that gives us clear direction and purpose!

   What causes our aimless wandering? The continuous rehearsal of old memories, hurts, and pains from our lives? The Bible says we are to forget about what has happened in the past. We must forgive, forget, and surrender it all. Release it all.

   We can release it all to God! Yes, we can cast aside our cares and be fully free from oppression and pain. We must ask God to interrupt our thinking patterns and our unforgiveness. We must decide that we indeed have the mind of Christ, and through Him have the authority he has given us. It is time for "necessary endings," so that we can see and obtain the brand-new direction that God wants for us. With God, we do not have to wander aimlessly in the wilderness; we can make a new path forward.

Think Before You Act

DAY 44

Recently, I was reading in Proverbs about the wisdom of giving things careful thought. As we know, King Solomon was a very wise man. In Proverbs, he wrote Godly truths that are every bit as relevant to our lives today as they were when they were penned.

This scripture below teaches us about the importance of giving careful thought to the things that we do, and how we must ponder and think deeply so we can stay on the path God has for us.

Proverbs 13:16 says:

> "WISE PEOPLE THINK BEFORE THEY ACT; FOOLS DON'T—AND EVEN BRAG ABOUT THEIR FOOLISHNESS."

We must make time for the things of God. We must meditate on His word and seek Him first before anything else, and let Him dictate our paths. We must not let our feelings, our fleshly desires, or other worldly things influence us.

I heard a quote once that says, "If you want to kill a man's vision, give him two."

What does that mean?

We never want to get sidetracked on a vision or path that is not from the Lord, because we will miss out on the amazing divine plan that God has for us. The enemy will always dangle the bait and lie in wait, ready with the enticements of the world, so that he may distract us and get us off the path God has ordained for us! We must focus on God's vision.

When there are too many things occupying our attention, we lose our focus on the true goal. We lose our peace, we can find ourselves in a crisis, and confusion sets in. We ultimately lose our way and give up.

But, God is not the author of confusion. If you want wisdom, you must decide to go after it! It will take resolve and determination to stay focused on God's plan. When we focus and meditate on His word, we can zero in on His divine path.

God is a Man of His Word

DAY 45

When our lives are pleasing to God, we can live in such a bold confidence.

1 John 5:14-15 states:

> "AND WE ARE CONFIDENT THAT HE HEARS US WHENEVER WE ASK FOR ANYTHING THAT PLEASES HIM. AND SINCE WE KNOW HE HEARS US WHEN WE MAKE OUR REQUESTS, WE ALSO KNOW THAT HE WILL GIVE US WHAT WE ASK FOR."

We cannot believe or trust God with perfect confidence until we are in a perfect union with God. First, we must know Him fully and rely on Him.

There was always a perfect union between God and Jesus when Jesus walked the Earth. He would ask of the Father, and God would give him what he asked. The moment Jesus prayed, he knew, and had total confidence, that God would open the heavens for him.

What makes us lose our confidence in all that God can do? Is it disobedience that distances us?

When we step outside the will of God, and harden our hearts towards the things of the Lord, it becomes hard to hear and discern from God, before we know it, we have turned away from everything we know God is calling us to do. Our feelings and emotions get in the way, and they tell us it is too late to get back on track.

The shortest verse in the Bible is in John 11:35:

> "THEN, JESUS WEPT."

Jesus wept because, even though they had seen the many works that He had done, the people present at Lazarus' grave, even his close friend, Martha, still had unbelief in Him. Unbelief brings brokenness and sadness to the heart of Jesus.

God's promises never fail. Faith comes by hearing God's Word. We will never get anywhere if we continually depend on our feelings; His Word is infinitely better than our feelings! It is alive, and should be our source of bold and unlimited confidence. There is power for those of us who dare to believe!

God's Perfect Love

DAY 46

Philippians 1:9 says:

"I PRAY THAT YOUR LOVE WILL OVERFLOW MORE AND MORE, AND THAT YOU WILL KEEP ON GROWING IN KNOWLEDGE AND UNDERSTANDING."

Are we people of circumstances, or are we people of faith? Do we truly have great faith, or do we get troubled and fearful the second the wind blows in the wrong direction?

"God, I may not understand right now, but, I know that this must be used for good." I have said this phrase more times than I can even count.

Hindsight is 20/20. We can always look back at the adversities and the trials in our lives, and, from our new perspective, we can see God's faithfulness, His mercy, His grace, all moving us in a direction of unending strength, reliance, resilience, and assuredness. Looking back is the easy part! But, we must ask ourselves if our eyes were on Jesus when we were in the midst of it?

We must surrender all and live completely for the glory of God. It is love in our Lord that establishes us, strengthens us, and upholds us. His love makes us strong when we are weak, and enables us to continually stand in the difficulties of the day-to-day battles.

We must draw near to God, and seek Him in all things through prayer and worship, and by meditating on His word. If we do this, we will allow the love of God to penetrate every inch of our being. The Bible is God's Word! His love poured out to us! And, when we use it every day, God will draw nearer to us, and we will draw nearer to Him.

Let God finish what He has started in you. He who began a good work will complete it. Let us allow His perfect love to do a mighty work in us!

Trust God's Word

DAY 47

The Word of God is God breathed. What does His Word say?

In the Bible, Jesus said to Satan three times, "It is written," and Satan's schemes were defeated. There is great power in speaking God's Word. Jesus quoted the Scriptures (and so should we) because the Bible is the living Word of God. God's Words have power when you speak His Words in faith!

It is time to stop being our own masters of disaster! Often, it seems we run from one crisis to another, constantly expecting the other shoe to drop. We allow fear, anxiety, doubts, and guilt to torment us. We must get in the power of the Word!

Luke 10:19 states:

> "LOOK, I HAVE GIVEN YOU AUTHORITY OVER ALL THE POWER OF THE ENEMY, AND YOU CAN WALK AMONG SNAKES AND SCORPIONS AND CRUSH THEM. NOTHING WILL INJURE YOU."

Do you think that God would create us to be failures? Absolutely not! We are made to be victorious in Him! We are all God's children, and we are to walk the Earth with an absolute power to do great and mighty exploits for Him.

God has put in us unique capabilities that are supernatural. Our abilities in Christ give us the capacity to control and bring everything under the authority of Christ. We have complete authority and dominion over every scheme of the enemy.

Go and preach the good news of the kingdom of God and His righteousness, as Jesus did. We are to be like Jesus in the world.

The power of God can remake us, mold us, shape us, change us, and allow us to be transformed. God's Word can make us new in every way! Trust God's Word!

God Wants You Back

DAY 48

Has there been a distance between you and God?
Isaiah 59:1-2 says:

> "LISTEN! THE LORD'S ARM IS NOT TOO WEAK TO SAVE YOU, NOR IS HIS EAR TOO DEAF TO HEAR YOU CALL. IT'S YOUR SINS THAT HAVE CUT YOU OFF FROM GOD. BECAUSE OF YOUR SINS, HE HAS TURNED AWAY AND WILL NOT LISTEN ANYMORE."

But, God is calling us back to Himself. We must be reconciled with Him!

Yes, God forgives all of our sins when we repent and turn away from them, but, if we feel distant from God, we must search our hearts to see what God has been asking us to give up, to walk away from.

The enemy temps us with sin and iniquity, and we get tricked into believing what we are doing (disobedience and sin) is not that bad, but, sin is sin to the Lord.

Our faith is something we must fight to keep: The Bible says the violent will take it by force. No longer can we stand around complacent and let the enemy steal what Jesus died for us to have. If we get wrapped up in the chains of our sinful nature, we will drift so far from the Lord! We will no longer be able to hear Him. It is time to fight the good fight of faith!

Psalm 51:12 says:

> "RESTORE TO ME THE JOY OF YOUR SALVATION,
> AND MAKE ME WILLING TO OBEY YOU."

Ask God to help us know His will, ask Him to give us spiritual wisdom and great understanding, and ask Him to help us live honorably, in a way that is pleasing to Him. God's secret plan is "Christ lives in us!" If He lives in us, then we never need to be distant from Him. We have the Holy Spirit in us to guide us and bring us back to that first place where we experienced the joy of our salvation. Repent! Turn back to Jesus!

Happiness Versus Joy

DAY 49

Happiness versus joy: What is the difference?

The word "happiness" brings about visions of unwrapping gifts on Christmas morning, park strolls with loved ones, and surprise birthday parties planned by all our closest friends. Or, perhaps it is finally buying that thing we have wanted; the thing we *thought* would make us happy.

Everyone wants to be happy. We pursue, and search endlessly for, happiness. We make it a lifelong mission to chase this elusive ideal. We spend money we do not have, collect things we do not need, and search for new and exciting ways to fill the void, just to bring us temporary happiness.

Unfortunately, this cycle will never end. If happiness depends on our circumstances, what happens when our gadgets break down, when our money is gone, when our loved ones die, or when our health deteriorates? It will be a constant cycle of disappointment. Happiness often leaves just as fast as it got there, and despair can set in just as quickly.

In contrast to happiness stands pure *joy*!

In Philippians 4:4, Paul says:

> "ALWAYS BE FULL OF JOY IN THE LORD.
> I SAY IT AGAIN—REJOICE!"

The secret to Paul's joy is grounded in his relationship with Christ, and it is available to each one of us. We desperately want to be happy, but we toss and turn over daily successes, failures, inconveniences, and pitfalls. Happiness depends on happenings, but joy unequivocally, wholly, and fully depends on Christ!

Running so much deeper and stronger, joy is the peaceful calm, quiet, and confident assurance of God's unending love and His powerful work in our lives. Joy is us doubtlessly knowing that He will always be there for us, no matter what!

If you have not yet made Jesus your Lord and Savior, call on His name today! We can receive the joy of the Lord, which will be our strength that changes everything. Let our endless pursuit of happiness end and begin anew at the same time with one word: Jesus. Call on His name!

Believe in Miracles

DAY 50

The Bible says we are to be like Jesus in the world. We are to walk in power, and do greater things than even He did, because we have full access to His complete love, supernatural power, undivided attention, and divine intercession.

Acts 1:8 states:

> "BUT YOU WILL RECEIVE POWER WHEN THE HOLY SPIRIT COMES UPON YOU. AND YOU WILL BE MY WITNESSES, TELLING PEOPLE ABOUT ME EVERYWHERE—IN JERUSALEM, THROUGHOUT JUDEA, IN SAMARIA, AND TO THE ENDS OF THE EARTH.'"

Our unending faith must make room for the extravagance of God. The lack of miracles, signs, and wonders causes the world to suffer! The world is crying out for something it does not even know it needs.

We are always praying for revival, but revival starts in each of us. Revival is an atmosphere for Christ's power to be manifested. If you are saved, a born-again child of God, then there have been signs and wonders in your life!

We want each of our lives to reflect the power of God working in us. The primary focus of our transformation (we are all miracles in the making!) is to reveal the nature of God within us. If there is no evidence of a new creation in the souls of Christians, then why would anyone want to be one?

We can walk in the evidence of God's glory! If we are to do greater things than even Jesus did, and if we have the power of the

Holy Spirit living in us, then why are we not seeing evidence of the miraculous every day?

We must have faith and seek God! And, as we seek Him, He will continually reveal to us great and mighty mysteries of His will. These revelations will help us to walk in His complete power, so we can live a life filled with the signs and wonders of Jesus. Walk in the glory of God in all you do!

Time to Enter the Promised Land

DAY 51

For years, God promised the Israelites a great inheritance.

In the 40 years the Israelites wandered the desert, generations came and went, but, the whole time, God met their needs with provision. They saw food fall from the sky. They witnessed the absolute brilliance of the parted sea, as they walked right through it, on dry ground.

Even after all these miracles, when they arrived at the walls of promised land, they deemed the giants inside to be too big for our God to handle. All *except* Joshua and Caleb; they saw how big their God was.

Numbers 13:30-33 says:

"BUT CALEB TRIED TO QUIET THE PEOPLE AS THEY STOOD BEFORE MOSES. 'LET'S GO AT ONCE TO TAKE THE LAND,' HE SAID. 'WE CAN CERTAINLY CONQUER IT!'

BUT THE OTHER MEN WHO HAD EXPLORED THE LAND WITH HIM DISAGREED. 'WE CAN'T GO UP AGAINST THEM! THEY ARE STRONGER THAN WE ARE!' SO THEY SPREAD THIS BAD REPORT ABOUT THE LAND AMONG THE ISRAELITES: 'THE LAND WE TRAVELED THROUGH AND EXPLORED WILL DEVOUR ANYONE WHO GOES TO LIVE THERE. ALL THE PEOPLE WE SAW WERE HUGE. WE EVEN SAW GIANTS THERE, THE DESCENDANTS OF ANAK. NEXT TO THEM WE FELT LIKE GRASSHOPPERS, AND THAT'S WHAT THEY THOUGHT, TOO!'"

Imagine finally walking up to the border of this mighty promised land, but, just as you are about to open the gate, you hear a voice that tells you you're too small, too *weak*, to defeat the giants?

My friends, God already knew about the giants! Do you think after all the years of God's promises that He was now going to say, "Oh, I'm sorry. I did not know about the giants. I guess you better turn back?" No! God does not make mistakes, and His plans do not fail.

Are you looking at Jesus, or at your giant? It is up to us how many years we want to spend in the wilderness by deeming our giants to be bigger than our God.

We must *believe* in order to enter the promised land. It is time to get what is ours, and what God has promised us!

Stand in Victory

DAY 52

Stand in Christ; He hears you!
Psalm 34:17-19 says:

> "THE LORD HEARS HIS PEOPLE WHEN THEY CALL TO HIM FOR HELP. HE RESCUES THEM FROM ALL THEIR TROUBLES. THE LORD IS CLOSE TO THE BROKENHEARTED; HE RESCUES THOSE WHOSE SPIRITS ARE CRUSHED. THE RIGHTEOUS PERSON FACES MANY TROUBLES, BUT THE LORD COMES TO THE RESCUE EACH TIME."

I love this scripture about how God will hear us and rescue us in times of trouble. And, my friends, it is not an if trouble comes, but when.

We live in a fallen world. We all face challenges every day in these difficult times, but, we will not get anywhere by running from everything that is hard in our lives. We also cannot expect God to deliver us all immediately from everything that is difficult or painful.

While God does not send us these storms, it is in these times of difficulty that we can grow in the absolute assurance of the faithfulness of the Lord. When trouble comes, we must take these opportunities to allow God's living Word to come alive in us. God uses these challenges in our lives to stretch our faith, to enlarge our vision, and to keep us focused on, and fully relying on, Him.

Apart from Him, we can do nothing. Sometimes, it takes our weakest moments in life to fully realize that! To stand strong during times of adversity, we need to put on the full armor of God, so that, when the day of evil comes, we can stand our ground! We can be victorious if we speak God's Words over our circumstances!

Find Rest in Him

DAY 53

God wants us to live a balanced life. Yet, for many of us, a balanced life seems so difficult to achieve. We spend our days juggling so many balls in the air that it is hard to find time to just relax, rest, and be in the presence of God.

But, that quiet place in the presence of our Lord is the only place where we can focus on He who has the ability to restore us and energize us. Rest is a weapon the enemy hates, he wants us to be weary and worn out.

Solomon 1:6 states:

> "DON'T STARE AT ME BECAUSE I AM DARK—
> THE SUN HAS DARKENED MY SKIN. MY BROTHERS
> WERE ANGRY WITH ME; THEY FORCED ME TO CARE
> FOR THEIR VINEYARDS, SO I COULDN'T CARE FOR
> MYSELF—MY OWN VINEYARD."

Is your life balanced? Or, are you neglecting your vineyard? We often find areas of our lives have been let go, *unkempt*, because we are too busy taking care of everyone and everything else.

The enemy comes to wear out the saints. If he can distract us with the constant issues of life, we can get off track and worn out. When we feel like this, it makes it hard to hear from God. God wants us to enjoy life, without constantly feeling exhausted and overwhelmed.

Each of us must decide to begin investing in ourselves, so that we are fully refreshed and ready to invest and minister to others around us. We must trust the Lord to rejuvenate and refresh us emotionally, spiritually, and physically. When we do this, we will begin to affect others positively, because we now have balance in our lives. We will begin to have a new joy, because that time with the Lord will strengthen us.

Begin to declare God's peace and victory over your life; spend time with Him, seek Him, know Him, and know His Word. Then, let God order your steps as you walk in the spirit, refreshed and ready for all that God has in store for you.

It Is All About the Cross

DAY 54

In the story of the Israelites in Exodus, God made a statute and an ordinance for them, and there He tested them.

Exodus 15:23-25 says:

> "When they came to the oasis of Marah, the water was too bitter to drink. So they called the place Marah (which means "bitter"). Then the people complained and turned against Moses. 'What are we going to drink?' they demanded. So Moses cried out to the Lord for help, and the Lord showed him a piece of wood. Moses threw it into the water, and this made the water good to drink. It was there at Marah that the Lord set before them the following decree as a standard to test their faithfulness to Him."

There are so many wonderful stories like this that show how the Lord took care of the Israelites while they were wandering in the wilderness. Repeatedly, situations arose that were scary, terrifying, and life-threatening. But, God always goes ahead of us, and He has a plan in place. He shows up when we cry out to Him and trust Him fully. When Moses cried out to God, God provided. Miracles happened! God always makes a way.

God knew that the waters would be bitter and unsuitable to drink, so He provided a *tree*. Yes, a tree was somehow growing in the middle of the desert, in this dry, parched wasteland.

Of course, God could have made the water fresh before they even approached it, but, God wants us to cry out to Him in times of trouble. He wants us to trust Him, and this requires action on our part in the form of faith. We must learn to trust God at His Word.

God provided the tree. God has already provided the tree we all need today: Jesus on the cross, nailed to a tree! Remember, no matter what you need, God has provided us with His one and only son, Jesus Christ. Jesus has come to make our bitter waters sweet.

Can You Hear God Knocking?

DAY 55

Once, I was waiting for someone to come to my house to do a repair. I was given a four-hour window, and was expected to wait around for him to show up.

While waiting, I got busy cleaning upstairs. I had music playing and did not hear the man knocking on my door. Apparently, he had been knocking for quite some time. But, because the time frame was earlier than the allotted window, I was not expecting him quite so early.

To make a long story short, I ended up getting a call from the repair company. They told me that he was at my door, and I was able to finally let him in. Even though I had prepared for his visit and rearranged my schedule, I may have missed it because I was not clearly listening!

I thought about that for a moment, and it seems that everything brings to mind something that God wants us to know. It made me question how many of us get so busy in our day-to-day routines that we fail to stop and listen to God knocking on the door of our hearts?

Revelation 3:20 says:

> "LOOK! I STAND AT THE DOOR AND KNOCK.
> IF YOU HEAR MY VOICE AND OPEN THE DOOR,
> I WILL COME IN, AND WE WILL SHARE A MEAL
> TOGETHER AS FRIENDS."

We pray and wait expectantly for God to show up, to *fix* something, but, after we have asked for help, do we then listen for His knocks? Do we listen for His promptings, guidance, wisdom, and His leading?

We must be ready to let God in! We must expect God to show up at any moment. God's timing is not our timing; His timing is perfect, because He knows things we do not yet know. Live every day of your life filled with the anticipation that God wants to bless you far above and beyond your wildest dreams. God is knocking. Will you answer?

We Have Been Given Power

DAY 56

My friends, we are in such need of Jesus. We need his presence, *and* we need the Holy Spirit, just like Jesus needed the Holy Spirit to fulfill his great missions.

John 14:12, Jesus says:

> "'I TELL YOU THE TRUTH, ANYONE WHO BELIEVES IN ME WILL DO THE SAME WORKS I HAVE DONE, AND EVEN GREATER WORKS, BECAUSE I AM GOING TO BE WITH THE FATHER.'"

If Jesus, being the son of God, was fully reliant upon his anointing from the Holy Spirit, then we should realize our desperate need for the Holy Spirit's presence to be upon us too. Only then can we be fully capable and equipped to do the assignments God has given us.

We can do absolutely nothing without the full power of the Holy Spirit working in us. Nothing! If we do not have the Holy Spirit living inside of us, then our lives will be a constant uphill battle. We will labor in vain. We will remain in the wilderness, never entering the promised land that is so steeped in victory. So, what's the point?

When you make Jesus your Lord and Savior, your life becomes naturally supernatural, because the Holy Spirit lives in *you*. He becomes your guide. When we give our life to Jesus, it does not mean our lives will be perfect; we will still have turmoil, trials, and suffering. But, we will have someone that will lead us, guide us, and deliver us through every trial!

It is time to let go of the religion, the rules, the checklists, and the "must-do's." We are to live, move, and have our being in Him. It is time to follow the anointing, and to walk in the power that belongs to us through salvation with Jesus Christ.

Take a Stand — DAY 57

Friends, how often do we fall for peer pressure? Or worry about being persecuted for our beliefs?

God wants us to stand strong! 1 Corinthians 16:13 states:

> "Be on guard. Stand firm in the faith. Be courageous. Be strong."

To stay strong, we must take a stand. No more situational ethics. No more doing what we *know* is wrong because of convenience, because it fits some narrative, or because it is what someone else wants to hear!

God does not want us to stay silent. Acts 18:9 says:

> "One night the Lord spoke to Paul in a vision and told him, 'Don't be afraid! Speak out! Don't be silent!'"

When we try to "keep the peace" to avoid getting stomped on by someone who is not following Jesus, we compromise our own peace. Yes, we can express what Jesus would do in a situation and refer to what the Word of God says; we do not have to fight or argue. But, saying nothing and doing nothing is not the way! When we feed into manipulation and control, it grows. Tolerance is not always a good thing if it goes against what God would have us do in that situation!

We need to do what is true and moral, no matter the cost. We cannot have a relative standard of morality. Commit to follow

God, and always lead, with the best of your ability in uncompromising integrity. Follow His Word, not what the fallen society would have you do!

Be a person after God's own heart. Do what is right, regardless of what the consequences are. Let God be your vindicator. Do not miss an opportunity to stand for Him!

What Does Jesus Think?

DAY 58

We may *think* we know what Jesus thinks, but do we?

Sometimes we think we know, but are we mistaken? This is illustrated in the Scripture in the story of the opposition of the Samaritans. When the people of the village did not welcome Jesus because he was on his way to Jerusalem, James and John called for rebuke, but, instead they were rebuked.

Luke 9:54 says:

> "WHEN JAMES AND JOHN SAW THIS, THEY SAID TO JESUS, 'LORD, SHOULD WE CALL DOWN FIRE FROM HEAVEN TO BURN THEM UP?' BUT JESUS TURNED AND REBUKED THEM. AND HE SAID, 'YOU DON'T REALIZE WHAT YOUR HEARTS ARE LIKE. FOR THE SON OF MAN HAS NOT COME TO DESTROY PEOPLE'S LIVES, BUT TO SAVE THEM.'"

Many of us think following religious rules and laws means following Jesus, but this is not necessarily the case. Religion is age-old in its destruction, and has often led to war; almost all of the wars in history were started, in one way or another, over religion.

We must get rid of our religion, our legalistic rules, our so-called "holy indignation." We get so puffed up and think we know it all, but we have no right to act in any manner that is in total contrast to the obedience of God's Word.

Remember, when Satan entered Judas, the devil could only speak through Judas to the priests of that time. The priests all conspired to get Judas to betray Jesus, and it was the devil, planting greed, that took money from these priests to put Jesus to death.

There is an age-old question that asks: What would Jesus do?

We must ask ourselves this every day, especially when we are tempted to act in strife, anger, and malice towards those who do not agree with us. The only one that can change others' hearts is Jesus! We must pray for our enemies and trust God.

What Does It Matter?

DAY 59

I have said this many times before, but I love when I am reading the Word and, suddenly, I experience a light bulb of revelation. I do not know why these moments continually surprise me. After all, God's Word is alive, and God always shows us exactly what we need to know all the time.

This happened to me while reading Philippians. Philippians 1:18 states:

> "BUT THAT DOESN'T MATTER. WHETHER THEIR MOTIVES ARE FALSE OR GENUINE, THE MESSAGE ABOUT CHRIST IS BEING PREACHED EITHER WAY, SO I REJOICE. AND I WILL CONTINUE TO REJOICE."

In the scripture above, it says "that doesn't matter." These words were penned by the apostle Paul while he was in prison. Paul continually states that the most important thing is to preach Christ, and for God's Word to spread, because when the final person has heard the good news, Jesus will return!

Aside from that, what else matters? We all get so entangled in the snares and cares of this world that we forget what truly matters: Us being with our Heavenly Father in paradise for eternity.

When we focus on our problems, instead of focusing on Jesus, our problems seem monumental. The enemy loves to dangle these distractions in front of us and turn mere hills into massive mountains. But, when we give our problems over to the Lord, these mountains will become level planes! It is all small to God.

When we look at things through the lens of Jesus, from His perspective, why should we even worry? The only thing that matters is that the gospel of the Lord Jesus Christ is preached throughout the world, and lives are changed and saved because of Him.

Magnify God

DAY 60

While reading through Romans, the following verse gave me pause.

Romans 1:21 says:

> "YES, THEY KNEW GOD, BUT THEY WOULDN'T WORSHIP HIM AS GOD OR EVEN GIVE HIM THANKS. AND THEY BEGAN TO THINK UP FOOLISH IDEAS OF WHAT GOD WAS LIKE. AS A RESULT, THEIR MINDS BECAME DARK AND CONFUSED."

Even though they knew God and had witnessed His miracles, the scripture says that they did not glorify Him or thank Him! Instead, they complained and grumbled, and they became vain in their imaginations. By acting this way, they diminished the hand of God, and stopped His impartation of blessings to flow in their lives.

It got me thinking: If we want God to *fully* operate in our lives, and if we want to walk in the ultimate impartation of the blessings that He has for us, then we better do the opposite of what the Romans did!

It is time to adopt a new vision. God already knows the good plan He has for us; let us get our thinking in line with His and avoid constantly envisioning the negative.

Instead, we must use our imaginations in a positive way. We must see ourselves victorious in Christ, and imagine our families thriving, our marriages restored, and our businesses and finances abundantly flourishing. We must see that the answers are all "yes" and "amen" concerning God's will in our lives.

It is time to magnify God above all! It is time to get our hopes up again, stop limiting God, and stop stalling our blessings with our complaints.

Give God glory, and exalt Him above all things by giving Him continuous heartfelt and loving praise. Believe God's Word over the word of man, and glorify Him above all else!

You Can Have What You Say

DAY 61

Most of us are familiar with the Bible's story of the woman with the issue of the blood. For twelve years, she suffered from constant bleeding, and this disability crippled her life.

But, when she saw Jesus, everything changed. Mark 5:28-29 says:

> "FOR SHE THOUGHT TO HERSELF, 'IF I CAN JUST TOUCH HIS ROBE, I WILL BE HEALED.' IMMEDIATELY THE BLEEDING STOPPED, AND SHE COULD FEEL IN HER BODY THAT SHE HAD BEEN HEALED OF HER TERRIBLE CONDITION."

You see, when she touched the garment of Jesus, she received exactly what she said! This story, like many others in the Bible, shows us that we can have what we say. This is true whether we speak good or bad, so we must be mindful of what we speak.

In Numbers 13, the children of Israel sent twelve spies into Canaan. Ten of the spies brought back a negative report from the promised land, while two of them brought back a positive report.

They all agreed that the land was flowing with milk and honey, but, ten of them warned of giants. They felt they were too small and insignificant to be able to defeat them. And, these ten spies got exactly what they declared: Not one of them were able to enter the promised land, and they remained in the wilderness until they died. What they said came to pass!

How many of us stop short of the promised land because of a "but?" You see, God already knew about the giants; God sent them there, and wanted them to look through the eyes of faith.

Remember we can have what we say. We must have a confession of faith, not doubt. It was not the giants in the land of Canaan who defeated the ten spies: They were the ones that defeated themselves!

Stop declaring failure. Instead, speak victory over your situations, and declare that our God is well able!

Be Encouraged

DAY 62

In times of trouble, it is easy to feel alone and discouraged. Psalm 10:1 says:

> "O LORD, WHY DO YOU STAND SO FAR AWAY? WHY DO YOU HIDE WHEN I AM IN TROUBLE?"

When we feel this way, we must consider what sermons we are preaching to ourselves. Why? Because our sermons will deem the course of our lives. As the mind thinks, the man follows!

Sometimes, we can be our own worst enemies. Can you imagine what God thinks of some of the sermons that we preach to ourselves?? The sermons of "I am not good enough, I've done too much wrong, I will never amount to anything, nothing ever goes right for me," and the list goes on!

Many of us sound like a broken record, but it is time to break that record and sing a new song. The Bible tells us that what we think, and what we say should be pleasing and acceptable to the Lord. It is time for a new "self-sermon!" It is time we stop living according to our situations and start living by revelation.

We must have a revelation of who is in the fire with us: Jesus! With Jesus, we are the majority. It is time to start finishing Satan's sermons with God's sermons of grace. Breakthrough, healing, restoration, provision? Grace is always the unmerited favor that blesses us. Understand and believe that Jesus already died for all that we will ever need. Know that it is already ours, because we are the righteousness of God in Christ!

Stop being so complacent in life, and growing used to things as they are now: You are not stuck there! God has a better plan for your life, and it starts when you encourage yourself in the Lord. Be encouraged!

Not Everything is an Attack from the Enemy

DAY 63

I have worked in ministry for many, many years, and one thing I often hear people say is: "I'm being attacked. This is an attack of the enemy!"

Recently, I heard a young woman say, "I plugged my phone in all night long, but I woke up and it was not charged... The devil just keeps messing with me!"

My friends, that is not the devil, that is a bad phone charger! We must stop giving the devil credit for everything!

To start, we must stop believing the lies about the devil. He is not omniscient or omnipresent, and he does not see all or know all like our loving Father does. The devil only knows what we say; he only can mess with what comes out of our mouths, what we declare about ourselves and our situations. By speaking negatively and declaring these things in our own lives, we are essentially giving him a foothold, an opportunity to take what we have said and run with it!

On this side of Heaven, it seems that we make the enemy out to be a pretty big deal, and I am certainly not discounting his plots and plans. But, when we magnify our God, and fully comprehend that He is well-able to brilliantly handle any and all darts the enemy launches our way, we can have victory. We have the Holy Spirit living in us, and it is He who is ever present.

With just one word of God, or just a mention of the name of Jesus, the enemy has to flee!

James 4:7 says:

> "SO HUMBLE YOURSELVES BEFORE GOD.
> RESIST THE DEVIL, AND HE WILL FLEE FROM YOU."

It is written!

Let us spend more time believing what God has said, and what Jesus has already done for us, instead of believing the enemy's lies. Either way, we must have faith in one direction or the other. Let us choose faith over fear!

It Is Time to Lead

DAY 64

God is calling all leaders!

How often do we find ourselves accepting certain situations because we do not feel like we have a choice in the matter? Often, we find ourselves living our lives, but not leading our lives.

The thing is, we *do* have a choice in the matter.

Nehemiah 2:17-18 says:

"But now I said to them, 'You know very well what trouble we are in. Jerusalem lies in ruins, and its gates have been destroyed by fire. Let us rebuild the wall of Jerusalem and end this disgrace!' Then I told them about how the gracious hand of God had been on me, and about my conversation with the king.

They replied at once, 'Yes, let's rebuild the wall!' So they began the good work."

Here, Nehemiah certainly had a choice to make. He was faced with accepting the situation at hand or changing it, and he made the decision to lead. God called him to lead, and He is calling us to lead, too!

Leadership is about making disciplined choices, choices that, many times, have a strong natural enemy in passivity. The enemy loves to freeze us in our decisions. But, indecisiveness can paralyze us; we become so afraid of making the wrong choice or the wrong decision that we do nothing.

Sometimes, it is because we are hesitant to "get involved." We are afraid to challenge the status quo, or are afraid of putting in the hard work. But, we must remember that everything worth achieving is not always easy.

For Nehemiah, the wall and the work of God in Israel was worth a determined effort. It was not going to be easy, but he was determined to get up that hill and build that wall!

No one else can build your wall. No one else is born with your purpose, or can fulfill your destiny. It is time to make decisions that will make a difference. It is time to do what we know we are created to do!

When the Battle Chooses You

DAY 65

Often in life we hear this statement: "Pick your battles."

While I was raising my boys, there were so many times I would walk into their rooms and just have to turn around and close the door. Yes, the boys' rooms were messy, but, I decided early on that this was not going to be a continuous battle I would fight.

I felt I had to choose my battles. Instead, I wanted to make sure my boys were walking with the Lord, getting good grades, and respecting authority. These battles were much more important battles than a messy room.

Yes, we should pick our battles. But, what happens when a battle chooses you?

It is not always our choice. Imagine getting a call that your child has been in an accident, receiving a bad doctor's report, or finding out a loved one has passed. These are battles we did not choose, yet they are still ones we must fight from time to time.

Too often, we only start praying in the midst of our trials. We turn to God in hope of a way out. But, the Bible tells us to put on the full armor of God so that we are always ready for whatever may come our way! If we are fully armed with God's Word, we can pray a hedge protection around us and our loved ones that is so strong that the enemy complains about it.

Job 1:10 says:

> "YOU HAVE ALWAYS PUT A WALL OF PROTECTION AROUND HIM AND HIS HOME AND HIS PROPERTY.

You have made him prosper in everything he does. Look how rich he is!"

God's Word is our battle plan, so we must know it and study it. It is what brings us out the other side stronger and victorious. We must be armed and ready. When the battle chooses you, you will have all you need in Christ to fight and win.

What Has God Given You?

DAY 66

How many times do we discount what God has already given us? In scripture, there is a story of a widow who is left with her husband's debt. She cannot repay the creditors and grows fearful that her sons will be taken away as slaves for repayment.

In a panic, she reaches out to Elisha for help. 2 Kings 4:2 states:

> "'What can I do to help you?' Elisha asked. 'Tell me, what do you have in the house?'
>
> 'Nothing at all, except a flask of olive oil,' she replied."

I find it interesting that Elisha asks one question, and then immediately follows it with the second. He did not give her a chance to answer the first question before moving onto the next. Why? My guess is because he did not want to hear her proclaim her story about what she did not have, deepening her fears in the process, but, instead wanted to switch the focus to what she did have.

I also find the widow's reply interesting: She answered that she had a small jar of oil, but, first, she said "nothing," Something she considered "nothing" was about to become a huge blessing in her life! Because she had faith, this small jar of oil turned into an unlimited supply that allowed her to pay off her debts and provide for her future.

The more we proclaim our deficits, the more real they become. God can always work with whatever we have when we are grateful.

God wants us to realize what we already have. He has not stopped being a God of miracles! Our miracles are in our hands! Let us allow God to multiply and bless what He has already given us.

Take Your Authority Back

DAY 67

In life, it is only natural for us to encounter others we disagree with, or consider "adversaries." However, it is important to remember that they are humans, just like us.

Our number one enemy is Satan. It is he who takes form in many ways and spreads evil over the world today. We know Satan is evil, and we cannot let him lead us into temptation to commit sins, or be filled with fear, anger, and unforgiveness. We must take back our authority!

After being baptized by John the Baptist, Jesus fasted for 40 days and nights in the wilderness. During this time, Satan appeared to Jesus and tried to tempt him. Jesus refused each temptation, so Satan departed, and Jesus returned to Galilee to begin his ministry.

We all know that Satan tries to wreak havoc in our lives by attempting to thwart the plans that God has for us. Notice that Jesus' ministry only began after He had the tools He needed to overcome Satan. But, guess what? We have those same tools of authority!

Before ascending to be seated at the right hand of the Father, Jesus told his disciples something important. Matthew 28:18 says:

> "JESUS CAME AND TOLD HIS DISCIPLES, 'I HAVE BEEN GIVEN ALL AUTHORITY IN HEAVEN AND ON EARTH.'"

Jesus assigned His authority to us! As born-again Christians, the power and authority of Jesus' name rightfully belongs to us, and He expects us to use it! We must take back our authority and turn to God to strengthen our will against all evil. Your victory has already been bought and paid for on the cross. Let us remember who we are and to whom we belong!

Stay Strong in the Word

DAY 68

I believe the greatest deception is a watered-down gospel. Why? Because the tragic results are eternal.

In the Bible, Jesus says there will be two groups of people in the end times: One group Jesus calls few, and the other He calls many.

In Matthew 7:22-23, Jesus says:

> "ON JUDGMENT DAY MANY WILL SAY TO ME, 'LORD! LORD! WE PROPHESIED IN YOUR NAME AND CAST OUT DEMONS IN YOUR NAME AND PERFORMED MANY MIRACLES IN YOUR NAME.' BUT I WILL REPLY, 'I NEVER KNEW YOU. GET AWAY FROM ME, YOU WHO BREAK GOD'S LAWS.'"

Many of Christ's professed followers are being deceived. This is a very frightening truth because they know His name, and their "religious" activities *seem* to have the marks of genuine ministry, but, Jesus, with a broken heart, will declare to them, "I don't know you." Why? Because they live a compromised life, full of sin without repentance, maintaining that their sin is no longer sin because the Bible was written so long ago. They consequently change the gospel to fit their own agendas.

We find another warning in Hebrews 2:1-4:

> "SO WE MUST LISTEN VERY CAREFULLY TO THE TRUTH WE HAVE HEARD, OR WE MAY DRIFT AWAY FROM IT."

We cannot drift away from the Word. Evil is so rampant in the world that we, as well as our leaders in ministry, need to stay so strong and so steadfast in the truth. We cannot stray or blur the line in the sand. What we say may not always be popular, but know we are all going to give an account on judgment day for the things we did and the things we did not.

By saying nothing, we say everything! By watering down the gospel, and changing the words to fit today's narratives, we will fall away. We must be part of the few and stay strong in the Word, because there is only one way to heaven: Jesus!

Lay It All Down

DAY 69

With God, we stand on level ground.

Psalm 26:12 says:

> "NOW I STAND ON SOLID GROUND,
> AND I WILL PUBLICLY PRAISE THE LORD."

No matter how rocky the ground seems in our lives right now, and despite the mountains that we are facing, we must remember the ground always stays level at the foot of the cross. We need to stay there on that level ground. We must be unshakable in Christ, even if the ground is shaking around us.

The Bible says we are to confess our sins to one another. We never have to go it alone. Find a fellow believer to be your accountability partner, and let others see the faults and the imperfections in your life. We do not have to be perfect, and it is okay to be vulnerable. Be real! Be honest! Honesty and confession are what leads to deliverance.

The enemy loves secrets. He loves to shake the ground and bring chaos into our lives. But, we can share our struggles and be vulnerable with Jesus. He already knows our flaws! We can exchange our flaws for godly characteristics. We can repent and turn away from all things that are holding us back.

It is time to get back to the solid, even, smooth foundation; the level ground. This is where Jesus is! We are all recipients of God's grace, but let us all act as deliverers of God's grace, too, and extend His merciful grace.

Let us lay our burdens down at the foot of the cross, and walk away in complete peace and on solid ground. God's got it. It is time to lay it all down!

Let Not Your Heart Be Troubled

DAY 70

Let not our hearts be troubled; instead, let it be cross-examined by our Lord. If we move to know Him, and understand His Word, our hearts will be at peace.

Psalm 26:2 says:

> "PUT ME ON TRIAL, LORD, AND CROSS-EXAMINE ME. TEST MY MOTIVES AND MY HEART."

If we do not let our hearts be examined by the Lord, then how will we know if we have let in a bitter root or a hardness of heart towards God? When the Lord comes with a blessing or correction, or gentle conviction, we must make it a stepping stone. If not, we are ultimately receiving God's grace in vain, with troubled hearts.

He wants you to know Him. Where there is strife, there is every kind of evil, and we never lose so much as when we lose our peace. The Lord gently convicts because He wants us to draw closer to Him by abandoning the things that are hardening our hearts.

When we release those things, we essentially clear a pathway for God to move in our lives. This is the time that God wants you to change from your insufficient strength to His overflowing and abundant strength. He wants you to remember that He is always with you.

When we are in prayer, we must remember how near we are to the Lord. The Lord is ready to hear us, 24 hours a day, seven days a week. Be not afraid to ask God to show you all things, and to give you revelations about where you have strayed off track. God is on the throne, waiting to answer you, and He is waiting for you to call on Him and to seek Him first. Every day, we must seek Him first and draw nearer to Him! When we get to that place, peace and victory are within reach.

In Jesus Name

DAY 71

In John 16:23-24, Jesus says:

"'AT THAT TIME, YOU WON'T NEED TO ASK ME FOR ANYTHING. I TELL YOU THE TRUTH, YOU WILL ASK THE FATHER DIRECTLY, AND HE WILL GRANT YOUR REQUEST BECAUSE YOU USE MY NAME. YOU HAVEN'T DONE THIS BEFORE. ASK, USING MY NAME, AND YOU WILL RECEIVE, AND YOU WILL HAVE ABUNDANT JOY.'"

Jesus said to ask the Father in His name, and He said this just before he went away. While we can always tell Jesus how much we love and appreciate him, when it comes to praying, we must ask the Father through the Lord Jesus. There is no other way to pray.

In Ephesians 5:20, Paul says:

"AND GIVE THANKS FOR EVERYTHING TO GOD THE FATHER IN THE NAME OF OUR LORD JESUS CHRIST."

Paul is telling us that it is to the Father, not to Jesus, that we give thanks. The name of Jesus is the *access* to the heart of the Father. Jesus has ascended high, and He is seated at the right hand of the Father. He is now our mediator, our intercessor, and our advocate in our Lord! He stands between us and the Father.

When you desire to get an answer, follow the teachings of the Word: Pray to the Father in the name of Jesus!

When we ask, we must believe that we shall receive, and because of that, our joy will be made full and complete. We must maintain joy even before we see the prayers being answered, even before the manifestation comes. Pray with a heart full of knowing that God has heard you, that you came to Him with the power of His Son's name.

When we learn to pray, to stand believing in the power of fervent prayer in alignment with what God's Word says, our prayers will be powerful and effective. In Jesus' Name!

Freedom

DAY 72

Do you ever feel trapped by overwhelming adversity? My friends, know that with God, there is always a way out.

We see this in scripture.

Psalm 124:7-8 says:

> "WE ESCAPED LIKE A BIRD FROM A HUNTER'S TRAP. THE TRAP IS BROKEN, AND WE ARE FREE! OUR HELP IS FROM THE LORD, WHO MADE HEAVEN AND EARTH."

With God, creator of all that exists, there is no problem that is beyond His ability to solve; there is no circumstance that is too difficult for Him. We can always turn to our loving Creator for help in our times of trouble and need, and He will set us free. In the above verse, David compared this to a bird that is able to escape from a hunter's trap. God will always provide a way out; we just need to trust Him and look for it!

God has given us the power, through the Holy Spirit, to be able to be set free and made clean in Him, but first, we must recognize that we need to be restored. God would not tell us we could be redeemed if we were unable to do so... Remember, the enemy loves secrets. But, when we confess our sins, we are taking our secret sins that are hidden in the darkness and bringing them into God's marvelous light.

Philippians 4:13 states:

> "FOR I CAN DO EVERYTHING THROUGH CHRIST, WHO GIVES ME STRENGTH."

It is only through the Blood of Jesus that we can be set free. We must look for the exit door that God has for us, ask Him to show us strategies and plans, and give us the knowledge and strength we need to be delivered from the lies, tricks, schemes, strongholds, and bondage of the enemy! There is freedom in Christ!

Combating Worry

DAY 73

So many of us are filled with worry, anxiety, and unrelenting fear. Fear is especially tormenting. It is one of the biggest lies of the enemy; yes, fear is a liar! These lies keep us distracted and so focused on the worry (the deception of the moment) that we simply become useless and cannot do all that God has for us to do.

This is the reason why fear is such a widely used tool of Satan. Fear can be polarizing, leaving us at a complete standstill in our lives. But, there is hope. God wants to teach us how to be content, confident, and combat worry. In fact, the Bible says 365 times not to fear, worry, or be anxious.

God wants us to be at peace and joyful, because the joy of the Lord is our strength. God wants us to hear His word so clearly that it will immediately, and at the onset, overrule and override every enemy lie.

Let us remember "The Four R's," and take back our peace and our freedom:

Rejoice! Release! Rest! Respond!

Yes, rejoice! Even though Paul was in prison often, one of the famous verses he writes in Philippians, 4:4-8, says:

> "ALWAYS BE FULL OF JOY IN THE LORD. I SAY IT AGAIN—REJOICE! LET EVERYONE SEE THAT YOU ARE CONSIDERATE IN ALL YOU DO. REMEMBER, THE LORD IS COMING SOON."

We need to learn to praise God, even in the storms. If we only trust Him in good times, then is it really trust? No! Trust starts where logic fails; it is when we cannot see a way out on our own that we know we can turn to God and rejoice no matter what we are going through. When we rejoice amid our worry, we give God room to work!

So, let us remember to rejoice, release, rest, and respond. Find rest in Christ, and relax in Him knowing He's got it all!

Stand Firm

DAY 74

It is no accident that we, God's people, are here to be intercessors and call forth God's Words concerning what is going on in the world today. In times like these, we must be carefully diligent that we do not pray one thing and then speak other things that contradict our prayers and go against God's promises.

Ephesians 6:13 says:

> "THEREFORE, PUT ON EVERY PIECE OF GOD'S ARMOR SO YOU WILL BE ABLE TO RESIST THE ENEMY IN THE TIME OF EVIL. THEN AFTER THE BATTLE YOU WILL STILL BE STANDING FIRM."

The Bible tells us to stand firm! We must keep our confessions in the Lord without hypocrisy. The power and promises of God's Word don't stop because of a certain set of circumstances. The Bible says a double-minded man is unstable in all his ways. My friends, does your heart and head line up with God's word?

In Isaiah 29:13, Jesus charged the Pharisees with setting aside God's Word in favor of their own traditions. Jesus dismissed their worship because their hearts were not aligned with their lips.

Living faith and true worship require that the mouth and the heart be aligned. Faith must emanate from lips that draw from the depths of the heart. Confessing our faith is not reciting slogans; that is acting only out of a human tradition, not from the heart. Jesus says this tradition is potentially hypocritical. We are called to genuine praise and worship, not to be pretenders or hypocrites.

Let us stand firm and confess God's promises without hypocrisy, and speak what the Holy Spirit has truly spoken into our hearts. This will allow us to declare the true promises of God!

Pray

DAY 75

There is so much power in prayer! If we could truly understand what happens when we pray, we would never cease to do so.

Mark 11:24 says:

> "I TELL YOU, YOU CAN PRAY FOR ANYTHING, AND IF YOU BELIEVE THAT YOU'VE RECEIVED IT, IT WILL BE YOURS."

My friends, when we pray, the whole world must pay attention, because God moves on our behalf and sends angels on assignment. All of Heaven springs into action!

Yet, sometimes, praying can feel like a struggle. Often, when we pray, we do not know what to say, or feel that we have prayed the same prayer thousands of times. We may feel unworthy, or like God does not hear us. We sometimes get distracted by phones ringing, our own thoughts, or other worldly things.

Sometimes, we wish that God would just open Heaven, pour out his answers through the chaos, and tell us it is all going to be okay. But, God does spring into action when we pray!

Imagine, if you will, God's replies to our prayers:

When you just asked me that...
...I dispatched angels to be on assignment.
...I rearranged all the plans in the kingdom and set them in place for your victory!
...the darkness was severely diminished, and the power of the enemy was destroyed.

The very second we begin to pray, angels move mountains. And what God starts, he finishes. New tracks have been laid. Strategies and plans, steeped in the miraculous, will fall into place.

God hears! God not only wants us to see ourselves as recipients of His blessings, but He also wants us to know that we are carriers of His favor. Pray the Word and the solution, not the problem. Begin to speak what God says, not what the enemy is whispering. Pray unceasingly! Powerful things happen when we do.

God's Perfect Peace

DAY 76

Recently, I was reading Isaiah 26:2-3, which says:

"OPEN THE GATES, THAT THE RIGHTEOUS NATION
WHICH KEEPS THE TRUTH MAY ENTER IN.
YOU WILL KEEP HIM IN PERFECT PEACE, WHOSE
MIND IS STAYED ON YOU, BECAUSE HE TRUSTS IN YOU."
(NKJV, FOR CONTEXT)

While reading this, I was reminded that God is always trying to show us something. He tries to give us a Word for how we are feeling. While there are many great talking points in this scripture, what stood out to me, and made me want to research this more, were the words "perfect peace." What is the difference between peace and God's perfect peace?

When I researched the translation from Hebrew, I found the word "shalom," which means "nothing broken, nothing missing." I have heard that definition before, but, when the Word says that God will keep us in "perfect peace," He is implying everything that the word shalom implies. Shalom implies health, happiness, well-being, peace, and restoration.

When the Scripture tells us we can have perfect peace when our mind is fixed on God, it does not use the usual Hebrew word for mind, but rather a word meaning "imagination." Isaiah's thought is that he whose imagination (which is the seat and foundation of all plans and ideas) is firmly planted on God's word will enjoy shalom, or "perfect peace," in its entirety.

God is giving us the blueprint to have His perfect peace. Let us keep our mind fixed on Him! Let us focus on the things of God, the truth of God's Word, and keep our imaginations focused on peaceful things, not on the things that can bring about fear and dread! God would not tell us to keep our minds focused on Him if it would not bring a positive outcome. Trust God! Stay in His perfect peace, and watch Him move powerfully.

Make Room

DAY 77

Everything around us is in a constant state of change. Change shows up unannounced, and mostly uninvited, and never makes an appointment on our calendars. We all wish that God would just tell us to mark our calendars for when big changes are coming, but that is not the case.

We need to be willing to roll with the changes, all while keeping our hearts and minds focused on God. My friends, we need to make room for what God wants to do in this unprecedented moment of change. Remember, God is our constant; He will never change.

After Jesus' death and resurrection, the disciples, who had once roamed the towns and villages side-by-side with the living, breathing Jesus, now had to solely believe by faith in what they used to be able to see. They were, as we are, in an invisible covenant of having to trust in an unseen God. It was a new way of relating to God. They could no longer go to Jesus; they had to believe that Jesus would come to them.

Even though this change had to be difficult to comprehend, Jesus told them it would be better this way.

John 16:7 says:

> "BUT IN FACT, IT IS BEST FOR YOU THAT I GO AWAY, BECAUSE IF I DON'T, THE ADVOCATE WON'T COME. IF I DO GO AWAY, THEN I WILL SEND HIM TO YOU.'"

Can you imagine what they were thinking? How could it be better that Jesus, the son of God, who previously taught them, walked with them, loved them, and worked mighty miracles all around them, was not only leaving them, but that His leaving would be more beneficial to them?

But, change has a purpose, and we must seek God for it!

When we pray and earnestly seek God in these times of uncertainty, God will bring us what we need. But, we need to make room in our hearts, and let go of the old wineskins, doubts, and past hurts. We must repent, pray, and begin to make room for all that God has for us in these times of great change!

Godly Wisdom

DAY 78

I feel now, more than ever, we need Godly and sound wisdom, so we can recognize evil and live victoriously in Christ..

The Bible speaks to the benefits of wisdom. Proverbs 2:9-10 says:

> "Then you will understand what is right, just, and fair, and you will find the right way to go. For wisdom will enter your heart, and knowledge will fill you with joy."

Our hearts are the place for the Commandments and God's Word to be kept. Wisdom is a gift from God! If we spent even half of the time learning His Word as we spend searching for worldly acceptance and gain, we would find something infinitely better: the Lord's wisdom.

God is the source of all wisdom, and His kind of wisdom brings peace. His knowledge is only accumulated by seeking Him. As we uncover the secrets of the Bible, we must be open to receive all God has for us and be filled with His knowledge. If we receive God's wisdom and apply it to our lives, we will do what's right in God's sight.

We are the righteousness of God in Christ. That is the greatest wisdom we can acquire; we are to have the mind of Christ.

The Bible says wisdom is more precious than rubies (Proverbs 8:11) and gold (Proverbs 16:16).

Words only become wisdom when they are put to use and allow the heart to change. This is a sacrifice only a few are prepared to make. But, wisdom identifies those who are true believers: those who seek to know, love, and obey God, and to live righteously. These covenant keepers alone will receive wisdom and experience God's protection. Do not just read the Word; do what it says, and be wise in Christ!

Faith Is in What We Cannot See

DAY 79

Faith is in what we cannot see.

Hebrews 11:1 says:

> "FAITH SHOWS THE REALITY OF WHAT WE HOPE FOR; IT IS THE EVIDENCE OF THINGS WE CANNOT SEE."

Most of us know the story of Jesus raising Lazarus from the dead in John 11, but, as I was rereading the story, I became aware in the supernatural, there is an order to things.

You see, while Jesus did receive word that Lazarus was terribly ill, He chose not to immediately go to His friend's side. When Jesus arrived, Lazarus was already dead. Jesus came to the area where Mary and Martha were, and He was deeply troubled by their sadness.

The sisters could not foresee or understand what was about to happen. They were looking at the situation logically: their brother was dead, and Jesus was too late to do anything about it. But, in all things, God will be glorified.

John 11:39 says:

> "'ROLL THE STONE ASIDE,' JESUS TOLD THEM. BUT MARTHA, THE DEAD MAN'S SISTER, PROTESTED, 'LORD, HE HAS BEEN DEAD FOR FOUR DAYS. THE SMELL WILL BE TERRIBLE.'"

How many of us miss the "set the stone aside" moments in our lives because we cannot logically understand His ways? Jesus' timing is not our timing. We are always in a hurry. We want Jesus to do things according to our logical thinking, but His ways are so much higher than ours. Though there are things we do not understand, we are called to believe, and to have faith that God knows things we do not.

Too many of us are praying and praising the Lord but not touching the stone! Let us not miss our miracle because of unbelief, or because we cannot logically see an answer. We must ask Jesus to send the help we need to get our stones rolling. It is time to be free and roll the stone aside! Have faith, and stop delaying God's power!

Let it Go

DAY 80

While reading about the Israelites fleeing Egypt, I always feel amazed that, while they so desperately wanted to escape and head to the promised land, many of them, in fear of the unknown, wanted to return to captivity.

Even as they were leaving captivity, the Israelites were not completely free, because they were still holding on to their old ways. Some even wished they could go back to Egypt, because it was all they knew; it was essentially their "normal," even though it was an awful way to live. What lied ahead for them was a total unknown, and many gripped onto the past, even though it meant being enslaved.

For the Israelites, accepting their freedom would be an ongoing process. Growing in God is an ongoing process, too; it is one that requires releasing something in order to receive something else. How many of us are continually staying in a job we hate, or maintaining an evil peace within our home or relationships, because we are afraid to be alone, or afraid to not be loved? But, we must not be afraid to let go of the bad because we think bad is good enough!

Exodus 14:5 says:

> "When word reached the king of Egypt that the Israelites had fled, Pharaoh and his officials changed their minds. 'What have we done, letting all those Israelite slaves get away?' they asked. So Pharaoh harnessed his chariot and called up his troops.

He took with him 600 of Egypt's best chariots, along with the rest of the chariots of Egypt, each with its commander."

Like in the scripture above, the enemy always seems to use the best forces to go after the people who are carrying the greatest anointing. If you feel like a lot is coming against you, that just means He has so much in store for you.

We have a choice in how we view things. Every day, we get to decide what we allow in our lives, and when it is time to stop letting the enemy control our thoughts. We can decide now to work with God or against God. Breakthrough comes from letting go!

Check Yourself

DAY 81

It is time to check ourselves!
2 Timothy 3:1-2 says:

"You should know this, Timothy, that in the last days there will be very difficult times. For people will love only themselves and their money. They will be boastful and proud, scoffing at God, disobedient to their parents, and ungrateful. They will consider nothing sacred."

In the above scripture, Paul's reference to "the last days" reveals his sense of urgency. The last days began after Jesus' resurrection, and the last days will continue until Christ's return. This means that we, too, are living in the last days, and we should make the most of the time that God has given us here on Earth.

Because we never know when Christ will come back, we must check ourselves daily, and be ready and vigilant. We should check our lives against Paul's list, so we do not give into society's pleasures and temptations.

Why is it so tempting to love pleasure rather than God? Sin is fun for a season, but it is a snare, a trap from the enemy. We may not immediately see the consequences of sin, which makes us think we have gotten away with something. But, God will not be mocked. Rest assured: God sees everything, and He knows our hearts! He knows if we really want to change.

We, as believers, must continuously grow in our knowledge of the Word, because ignorance can make us vulnerable to deception. We must not sin and repent, sin and repent—we must stand! We must stand up against evil by living as God would have His people live.

God is using all of us to raise the standard against all evil. We must check our hearts and our minds, and we must pray more than we complain. Let us speak the Word over evil. We are in the world, but not of the world.

Calling All Watchmen

DAY 82

The Lord is calling on the watchmen! Isaiah 62:6 states:

> "O Jerusalem, I have posted watchmen on your walls; they will pray day and night, continually. Take no rest, all you who pray to the Lord."

The true spirit of prayer is watchfulness and restlessness. Being a watchman means being "on the Lord's watch." Isaiah calls intercessors watchmen, noting that they are positioned high on the walls. With such a great perspective, they have an advantage to view and to be prayerfully focused in three directions: in the physical, here and now; among the nations; and towards developments in Heaven itself.

God has made us, His people, to be His watchmen!

Watchmen take stock of all that is going on with a spirit of urgent restlessness, refusing to keep silent before God! To be His watchmen, we must be diligent in prayer, go to the throne room of God on our knees, and cry out to God for all that we need. We, all together, can be the standard God uses against the enemy.

God says if His people would repent and turn away from their sins, He will hear our cries from Heaven, and will heal us and restore our land. We must pay attention—the enemy comes like a thief in the night, seeking those who he can destroy.

It seems like Christianity is under siege. Our very free society and freedoms are under attack. Everything seems quite different now, and it is all happening under our very noses. The enemy hides in plain sight!

Let us be the watchmen: prayerful and part of the solution. We are all going to give an account for the things we did do while on Earth, but, I also believe we will give an account for the things we did not do!

Let us sound the alarm, and let our battle cries be heard in Heaven!

Jeremiah the Prophet

DAY 83

Perhaps more than any other book in the Bible, the book of Jeremiah reveals a prophet's inner wrestling. I love the example of the prophet Jeremiah, because, even though he had both a strong anointing and inner struggles with the call on his life, he did not back down, no matter his inhibitions.

In Jeremiah 11:6-7, the Lord tells Jeremiah to relay the following message to Judah:

> "Then the Lord said, 'Broadcast this message in the streets of Jerusalem. Go from town to town throughout the land and say, 'Remember the ancient covenant, and do everything it requires. For I solemnly warned your ancestors when I brought them out of Egypt, 'Obey me!' I have repeated this warning over and over to this day.'"

Can you imagine the anguish he had over delivering the message of judgment upon the people, and the coming destruction of the land? Jeremiah would confess candidly the inner turmoil he had concerning his call to prophetic ministry. Yet, no matter what, he fulfilled his calling proclaiming God's judgment against the people of Judah and their lack of faithfulness to God.

Jeremiah remained so faithful to God, despite his countless hardships and trials.

Do we remain faithful amid hardships? Or, do we jump ship as soon as we think God has not answered us in the way or in the timing that we would have liked?

Jeremiah's dialogues, prayers, and confessions reveal such a deep understanding that this prophet had regarding God's love, character, and faithfulness. For Jeremiah, there was absolutely no doubt that God was who He said He was: the God of all creation!

Jeremiah's warning was not only a message of judgment, but also of hope. He told of promises that a righteous remnant would be restored! Just like he was calling Jeremiah to sound the alarm, God is sounding an alarm today for us. Let us stand together and pray that God would indeed restore, bless, and heal our land as we repent and turn away from sin and unrighteousness.

Do You Know Jesus?

DAY 84

Everything changes when Jesus walks in the room. There is absolutely nothing like His presence.

Jesus came to set the captives free. This means we, too, can be free. We can be free from sin, worry, pain, anxiety, and fear. Being a Christian does not mean the absence of troubles: we live in the world, and, in the world, we do have troubles, but, being a born-again Christian means that Jesus will be with you through it all.

John 3:5-7 states:

> "Jesus replied, 'I assure you, no one can enter the Kingdom of God without being born of water and the Spirit. Humans can reproduce only human life, but the Holy Spirit gives birth to spiritual life. So don't be surprised when I say, 'You must be born again.'"

God has an amazing plan for your life, and, with Jesus, you will never have to go it alone. When He comes into your heart, He stays there. He will never leave you or forsake you, and you will spend eternity with Him in Heaven. There could never be a better plan! If you are not living God's plan, call on the name of Jesus today and be saved. Know that you are going to Heaven when you die, because eternity is a long time to get this wrong.

Say this prayer, and mean it with your whole heart:

Jesus, I repent of my sins. I know that you bled for me and died for me, and were raised from the dead. Please, forgive me of all my sins. I ask you to come into my heart, and I will make you my Lord and Savior!

Stay in the Word, and know that God will begin to speak to you through His Word, and you will be changed through the power of the blood of Jesus Christ!

Grace, Grace, and More Grace

DAY 85

What is God's grace, and why do we need it?

Grace is...

... a way of moving that is smooth and attractive.

... a controlled, polite, and pleasant way of behaving.

... to confer dignity or honor on.

We need God's grace! I, for one, am so grateful for God's grace every day. The Bible says we all fall short of God's glory each day, and, therefore, we need such grace. The unmerited favor is the very thing we do not deserve. Grace cannot be earned, but it is given to us liberally through the love of Jesus Christ.

Ephesians 2:8-9 states:

"GOD SAVED YOU BY HIS GRACE WHEN YOU BELIEVED. AND YOU CAN'T TAKE CREDIT FOR THIS; IT IS A GIFT FROM GOD. SALVATION IS NOT A REWARD FOR THE GOOD THINGS WE HAVE DONE, SO NONE OF US CAN BOAST ABOUT IT."

God's grace is what allows us to get through the difficult times with a spirit of ease and an unshakable sturdiness. It is knowing we are not alone, and that the Holy Spirit goes with us always. Grace means that we have the help of all of Heaven, and we have ministering and warring angels continuously by our side, helping us fight the good fight of faith. Grace means we are never alone, but that, when we know Christ, we are one with Him, and we continuously have the help of all of Heaven as our rear guard, our safety net, and our edifier. Thank you, Lord, for your grace!

2 Corinthians 12:9-10 states:

"Each time, he said, "My grace is all you need. My power works best in weakness." So now I am glad to boast about my weaknesses, so that the power of Christ can work through me. 10 That's why I take pleasure in my weaknesses, and in the insults, hardships, persecutions, and troubles that I suffer for Christ. For when I am weak, then I am strong."

Commit Your Way

DAY 86

Commit to the Lord, and He will bring it to pass. We must refuse to play games to get ahead in society; God will promote us! If we compromise our beliefs, we will never be happy. Do not justify things that our conscience condemns; we will all give an account for what we have done in our lives, and for the things we have not done that God has called us to do.

When we get to the gates of Heaven, we will most certainly be held accountable. Remember, we are God's heirs, and we are to share His sufferings if we are to share His glory. So, always do what is right, even when you do not feel like it.

James 1:5-8 says:

> "IF YOU NEED WISDOM, ASK OUR GENEROUS GOD, AND HE WILL GIVE IT TO YOU. HE WILL NOT REBUKE YOU FOR ASKING. BUT WHEN YOU ASK HIM, BE SURE THAT YOUR FAITH IS IN GOD ALONE. DO NOT WAVER, FOR A PERSON WITH DIVIDED LOYALTY IS AS UNSETTLED AS A WAVE OF THE SEA THAT IS BLOWN AND TOSSED BY THE WIND. SUCH PEOPLE SHOULD NOT EXPECT TO RECEIVE ANYTHING FROM THE LORD. THEIR LOYALTY IS DIVIDED BETWEEN GOD AND THE WORLD, AND THEY ARE UNSTABLE IN EVERYTHING THEY DO."

Do not be unstable! We must always think, pray, and ponder the things of God before we make big decisions. Do not make decisions based on emotions, because desire uses our emotions to deceive us. Ask God, and seek His confirmation in all things.

The Bible says that God has written a plan for each of our lives before we have ever lived a day. We are humans, and our plans are flawed. God's plan is perfect; He sees the obstacles before we ever encounter them, and He has already made a way around it all. Wait on His perfect timing.

Apart from God, we can do nothing! Yes, no matter what we have been through in our lives, or what we are currently going through, God alone can turn our entire situation around in an instant and use it for good. Times like this are not the times to run from God, but to instead throw yourself at His feet and trust Him! Commit your way!

God Is For You

DAY 87

Jesus is who He says He is, and He will never change. If Jesus leaves the flock of 99 to go after the lost one, you know he won't stop until that lost sheep is found. Yes, it seems illogical that Jesus would leave 99 sheep all alone just to go after the lost one; it does not make any sense —unless the one that is lost is you, or someone you love. It is not His will for anyone to perish.

Jesus wants a close personal relationship with us. We will never be lost or alone when we have Jesus in our lives! But, when we are walking in a close personal relationship with the Lord, the enemy of our souls tries to tear the relationship down at every turn.

Isaiah 54:17 says:

> "BUT IN THAT COMING DAY NO WEAPON TURNED AGAINST YOU WILL SUCCEED. YOU WILL SILENCE EVERY VOICE RAISED UP TO ACCUSE YOU. THESE BENEFITS ARE ENJOYED BY THE SERVANTS OF THE LORD; THEIR VINDICATION WILL COME FROM ME. I, THE LORD, HAVE SPOKEN!"

Put almighty God up against any evil and watch Him fight for us! We must be vigilant and recognize the tactics of the enemy, and combat them with the God's Word. No person, no evil, no lie, no slander, no infirmity, and no weapon formed against us can ever prosper. If God is for you, then who would dare be against you? Time is up for the enemy.

We will run our race with endurance, and put our total confidence and faith in He who holds all the answers, who will help us get to the finish line. There is nothing that will get by Him. God is with us, and He will never leave us. We will never be lost sheep again when we have Jesus as our Lord and Savior.

Time is up for the enemy; it is game over! He has been found out! He is a defeated foe! We will all run our race with endurance. We are all here for such a time as this. No matter what you are going through, choose to trust God. Put your total confidence and faith in The One who holds all the answers. He will get you to the finish line. Remember: He is the author and the finisher of our faith, and there is nothing He won't do for you.

At Home with Mary and Martha

DAY 88

Luke 10:38-42 tells the story of Jesus visiting the home of Mary and Martha:

"As Jesus and the disciples continued their way to Jerusalem, they came to a certain village where a woman named Martha welcomed Him into her home. Her sister, Mary, sat at the Lord's feet, listening to what He taught. But Martha was distracted by the big dinner she was preparing. She came to Jesus and said, 'Lord, doesn't it seem unfair to you that my sister just sits here while I do all the work? Tell her to come and help me.'

But the Lord said to her, 'My dear Martha, you are worried and upset over all these details! There is only one thing worth being concerned about. Mary has discovered it, and it will not be taken away from her.'"

In this story, Martha was so caught up in her "work" that she missed out on what was truly important: His Word. But her sister Mary didn't miss a thing; she sat at Jesus' feet to soak up every bit of His knowledgeable and loving teachings. Nothing was more important to her than seeking Him and being in His presence.

How many times do we let a "good" thing get in the way of the "greatest" thing?

In this story, do you think Jesus expected a perfectly clean house, an elegantly set table, and a gourmet meal of the finest cuisine? No, certainly not. He was more concerned about the people gathered for dinner than the dinner itself. This is true in our lives, too.

I imagine Martha looked back at the situation and wondered how much she had missed by worrying about the details. I wonder how long she stayed angry with her sister for not helping, allowing strife into her life.

Do not make the same mistake as Martha: Let us always respond to the absolute miracle of being able to know God personally. We must make time for God and put Him first always! Only then shall we have all other things.

Through a personal relationship with God, we can walk in His perfect peace!

God Wants You Well

DAY 89

Jesus did not die for believers to remain bound by illness, sickness, and disease. We are not meant to be bound by depression, fear, and anxiety! Jesus' blood and His death on the cross already paid for our healing and deliverance.

He has risen and is seated at the right hand of His Father, interceding for us. Yes, Jesus is praying for each of us. When we understand that healing is already ours, and we believe it with our whole hearts, we can have what we ask according to God's will!

Psalm 34:17 says:

> "THE LORD HEARS HIS PEOPLE WHEN THEY CALL TO HIM FOR HELP. HE RESCUES THEM FROM ALL THEIR TROUBLES."

There is not one sickness, not one disease, that Jesus does not have complete authority over. We need to remember who our Father is. As children of the Lord, we can walk in divine peace and divine health, knowing God wants us well. He sent his son Jesus to pay the price for anything we could ever need, which means the spirit of infirmity cannot come to steal, kill, or destroy.

Why wait to take authority over sickness and flu until it hits your house? Declare and decree to bind and break all infirmity, sickness, depression, fear, and anxiety from entering our body, household, and territory. Order the spirit of oppression, infirmity, and anxiety go in the name of Jesus Christ!

Jesus came so that we might have life so we would live that life to the fullest! Let us take our freedom over all our worries and cast them off and onto the mighty, powerful, and healing hands of our loving Father.

At the name of Jesus, all sicknesses and depressions and anxieties must flee. Glory to God; we have complete authority!

1 Peter 2:24 says:

"HE PERSONALLY CARRIED OUR SIN IN HIS BODY ON THE CROSS SO WE CAN BE DEAD TO SIN AND LIVE FOR WHAT IS RIGHT. BY HIS WOUNDS, YOU ARE HEALED."

God Wants Your Soul Healed Now!

DAY 90

Does it ever feel like you have hit your absolute bottom?

I sense this is what is going on with many believers today. I feel it in my heart, and in my family as well.

3 John 1:2 states:

> "DEAR FRIEND, I HOPE ALL IS WELL WITH YOU AND THAT YOU ARE AS HEALTHY IN BODY AS YOU ARE STRONG IN SPIRIT."

Why is it so important for us to be strong in spirit, and for our souls to prosper?

When our souls prosper, we are set free and we can love others. We can be the light of Jesus in this world; we can begin to live and move and have our being in Him. We can keep His Commandments and live out our purpose in Christ.

To prosper, we must stay strong in spirit. The enemy tries to keep us in bondage and bring up past pain, our lingering pain that is hidden away deep in the recesses of our souls. But, there will come a day when the patches we lay to protect ourselves will just not work anymore. No more short-lived Band-Aids!

Our pain springs forth like weeds in a beautiful garden, and these weeds choke off all that is good. The enemy loves the weeds. But, it is time to declare that the love of Jesus can deliver us from our pain, our weeds.

It is time to dig down deep, deeper in our faith, to let the love of Jesus encompass and heal us. Friends, it is time to lay a new foundation and seal these old wounds forever. It is time for deliverance!

Declare right now that this is the last day you will spend in darkness believing the enemy's lies. You are coming into the light! You will live the life that Jesus Christ of Nazareth has died for you to have. Declare that your soul is healed now!

Put on Your Robe of Righteousness

DAY 91

Today's news is filled with chaos and confusion. We might ask ourselves how our world can be this turbulent and wayward, but, we must remember that God is not surprised by any of it.

Isaiah 61:10 Says:

"I AM OVERWHELMED WITH JOY IN THE LORD MY GOD! FOR HE HAS DRESSED ME WITH THE CLOTHING OF SALVATION AND DRAPED ME IN A ROBE OF RIGHTEOUSNESS. I AM LIKE A BRIDEGROOM DRESSED FOR HIS WEDDING OR A BRIDE WITH HER JEWELS."

The Bible talks about a time when evil is good and good is evil. This is exactly where we are right now...

I want to remind everyone that we, as believers, are covered in a beautiful robe of righteousness. What exactly does that mean?

Imagine this beautifully designed, supernatural robe of the finest fabrics and beautiful threading. I'm sure it will be very ornate, but, spiritually speaking, what will it have? Righteousness! We all have the righteousness of God in Christ, and that means final deliverance from fear, anxiety, addiction, infirmity, bondage, oppression, depression, and lack! Tucked into the many deeply lined pockets of this robe of righteousness, we will find divine health, prosperity, peace that surpasses all understanding, complete joy, and overwhelming victory!

Let's all wear this beautiful robe of righteousness, because that's who we are, through the blood of the lamb and the words of our testimony! WE WILL OVERCOME! Undoubtedly declare that God is still God, and He still has an amazing plan for our lives! We will see the goodness of the Lord here in the land of the living! Let's all stand together, praying and believing, as in Isaiah 61, that God's word is truth, and it will be as He has said.

God's Plan

DAY 92

Have you ever pondered God's ultimate plan for your life? Have you ever considered what your life would look like if you were to live the exact life God had planned for you? My friends, it is never too late to get back on the right path.

Proverbs 19:21 says:

> "YOU CAN MAKE MANY PLANS, BUT THE LORD'S PURPOSE WILL PREVAIL."

Before you ever lived a day on this Earth, you were born with an amazingly brilliant plan for your life, authored by God.

We are all still here, and we are here for such a time as this. We are to be God's watchmen on the wall. We are to hold the doorway open for the gospel. We are to stand for Christian values and for God's Word. Sometimes, God's plans are hard, and even painful, because it means leaving behind the status quo, but I promise, it will always be worth it. God knows how strong you are. God knows your heart for justice and truth.

God wants us all to sound the alarm, to be of one voice and stand for truth, peace, and freedom for all. The truth will set us free.

So, my precious friends, put your battle armor on and get ready to run. Let us all be part of the solution and live out our purpose and plan in Christ. We must be determined, stand for the truth, stand for Christ, and stand up for the gospel. When we give God all glory in all things, we will see God move like never before.

I pray the Holy Spirit fire falls in the name of Jesus. We will walk naturally supernaturally and see mighty miracles manifest. Behold, God is doing a new thing; can you not perceive it? It is God's plan.

When God Restores, He Multiplies

DAY 93

God restores! He does not just restore us to where we were before. When He restores, He multiplies! The enemy must repay us for everything he has stolen. God sees to it! That is a bonafide promise from the Lord.

I am reminded of the story where David and his men were off fighting battles and returned to find their homes burned down, and their wives and children missing. They wept in such utter despair. David was faced with such a horrific crisis, and all his men were turning on him and blaming him.

Can you even imagine finding your whole family missing, not knowing if they were dead or alive? Your whole town, burned to the ground. It would be extremely hard to see your way out of this catastrophe. The scripture says David encouraged himself in the Lord, and the Lord told him to not only go after the enemy, but to get what was stolen from them.

1 Samuel 30:8 says:

> "THEN DAVID ASKED THE LORD, 'SHOULD I CHASE AFTER THIS BAND OF RAIDERS? WILL I CATCH THEM?' AND THE LORD TOLD HIM, 'YES, GO AFTER THEM. YOU WILL SURELY RECOVER EVERYTHING THAT WAS TAKEN FROM YOU!'"

They did recover everything that was taken. They were able to get their family members back home safely, but they also got so much more. They recovered all the plunder that the enemy had stolen in past battles, as well as all their own goods. This is how our God works: He can restore and multiply all that the enemy has taken.

Declare your breakthrough and God's multiplication over everything you have lost, in Jesus' name. Restoration is coming. Declare it and receive it!

Overwhelming Victory

DAY 94

Today, I want to remind everyone the battle belongs to the Lord. We are not fighting for a victory, but, rather, we are fighting from a place of victory with Jesus. Yes, we are coming from a place of divine victory, and that victory is already yours in Jesus Christ, because the battle has already been fought and won by Jesus' powerful blood.

Romans 8:37 says:

"NO, DESPITE ALL THESE THINGS, OVERWHELMING VICTORY IS OURS THROUGH CHRIST, WHO LOVED US."

It is time to take our seat with Jesus at the right hand of our Father. We must imagine how it feels to sit in the throne room, with Jesus at the right hand of God, who sits from this mighty place of importance. We must let the enemy be the footstool under our feet, and, from this victorious place, we will rule and reign in life.

We must command our victory. Stop declaring defeat, but speak only the victorious outcome you desire. It is time to flourish and thrive, and declare victory in Jesus' holy name! In Jesus, we know no defeat. Let us declare victory after victory. Yes, indeed, overwhelming victory is ours in His name, and there is absolutely nothing that God will not do for us.

Deuteronomy 20:1-4 says:

"FOR THE LORD YOUR GOD IS GOING WITH YOU! HE WILL FIGHT FOR YOU AGAINST YOUR ENEMIES, AND HE WILL GIVE YOU VICTORY!"

Reach up and adjust your crown, and know that you have the help of all of Heaven backing you. Know that it is our rightful place, and a place of absolute victory, because we are children of the highest God.

Final Judgement

DAY 95

My friends, we need to wake up! There is a great awakening coming, and people are being greatly deceived. Suddenly, everything is offensive. So, we shrink back and keep quiet; we certainly do not want to offend.

It makes us ask: What does God want from us, and for us?

God wants us to thrive in our purpose to serve the kingdom of God as His ambassadors. Yes, this is a great commission for us all. The enemy prowls around like a thief in the night, deceiving souls through the temptation of sin and sheer complacency. Yet, we are so busy trying not to rock the boat that we keep to ourselves. We think that it is none of our business, and that it is better not to interfere.

But, we cannot stay complacent. After all, it does not matter what other people think—only what God thinks. If we are true believers of Jesus Christ, then we have a job to do, but, first, we need to ask ourselves tough questions: Are we determined that we know how to judge what is good for us? Are we deciding for ourselves if certain sins are acceptable?

John 3:36 states:

> "AND ANYONE WHO BELIEVES IN GOD'S SON HAS ETERNAL LIFE. ANYONE WHO DOESN'T OBEY THE SON WILL NEVER EXPERIENCE ETERNAL LIFE BUT REMAINS UNDER GOD'S ANGRY JUDGMENT."

If you do not want to obey His Word, Jesus is not yet the Lord of your life! We may think we can forgo God's Commandments and just call to Jesus on our deathbed, but the Bible says that God will then say that He "did not know you." This statement gives me chills. The Bible is clear that Jesus is the only way to spend eternity in Heaven with our Father and creator. We never know when our last day will be.

Are you prepared for final judgement? If you have not given your life over to Jesus, do it now! Life is too short to get this wrong. Through salvation, we must completely surrender everything, including our own judgement. Be a true disciple and be saved.

Have a Seat

DAY 96

Matthew 11:28-30 states:

> "THEN JESUS SAID, 'COME TO ME, ALL OF YOU WHO ARE WEARY AND CARRY HEAVY BURDENS, AND I WILL GIVE YOU REST. TAKE MY YOKE UPON YOU. LET ME TEACH YOU, BECAUSE I AM HUMBLE AND GENTLE AT HEART, AND YOU WILL FIND REST FOR YOUR SOULS. FOR MY YOKE IS EASY TO BEAR, AND THE BURDEN I GIVE YOU IS LIGHT.'"

Who else needs this scripture today? We must rest!

Rest is a weapon the enemy hates. He loves when we are weary, beaten down by the cares of the world, and exhausted from fighting the battles of the flesh.

But, when we spend time with God, we rest. In His Word, and in His presence, we do not need to be worried or exhausted. We do not need to be anxious or frustrated while we are waiting on Him and seeking answers from Him.

Sometimes, when we start to get on board the Worry Train, we just need to tell ourselves, "Sit down." We must be still. Letting our emotions and our anxieties spiral out of control can cause us to be on that fast-moving Worry Train for a long ride!

Do not board that train; instead, sit at God's feet and rest. That does not mean just your physical body; it also means your soul, your mind, and your emotions. Submit it all to God, because, apart from Him, we can do nothing.

He knows our worries and our fears, but, unless we cast our cares to Him, we will not understand how He wants to help us. Sitting with Him lets us hear His Word, so we can receive His plan. It is so unbelievably important to let your entire being be at rest!

Today, if you are struggling, take a seat, get in God's presence, and rest in His perfect peace. The promise of God's peace is not always made known to those who toil and strive in their own strength, but to those who sit and rest in the powerful presence of Jesus Christ. Wait on Him and your strength will be renewed!

It Has to be Used for Good

DAY 97

We must trust God, no matter what is going on around us. Romans 8:28 says:

"AND WE KNOW THAT GOD CAUSES EVERYTHING TO WORK TOGETHER FOR THE GOOD OF THOSE WHO LOVE GOD AND ARE CALLED ACCORDING TO HIS PURPOSE FOR THEM."

The Bible is full of stories that portray this scripture exactly. One of the best examples is found in Acts 27. Here, we find Paul and his crew shipwrecked. Jesus had instructed him to go to Rome to meet with Cesar, so we can imagine the distress he felt when he was suddenly stuck in a powerful storm at sea.

All 276 men on board had gone through a major battering from the unrelenting siege of powerful storms. They were left hungry, weak, cold, wet, exhausted, and scared. But, the Bible says that not *one* of them perished.

Not only was God protecting Paul, but everyone on that ship was protected because of the anointing and blessings on Paul! Paul believed in God and remained in faith, no matter how horrible his circumstance seemed.

While shipwrecked on the island of Malta, they met the islanders who lived there. The chief official was suffering from a life-threatening disease, but Paul prayed for him and he was healed, as well as the other sick people. The islanders were able to hear about and see the goodness of God! As a result, Paul and his crew were showered with honors and given supplies for the remainder of their journey.

You see, God had a plan: He used Paul mightily in a situation that had seemed like an impossible catastrophe, but it turned out to be an enormous and miraculous blessing that changed and blessed the masses in ways Paul never dreamed.

We must look for our blessings amid the trials, and declare His Word that says God will turn this around and use it for good. This is God's promise!

God's Hands

DAY 98

Have you ever thought about God's hands?

God's hands are the hands that create us, that rescue us, that hold us, that carry us, that lift us, that shelter us, and that comfort us. It is His hands that mold us, and His hands that love us.

Isaiah 41:10 says:

> "DON'T BE AFRAID, FOR I AM WITH YOU.
> DON'T BE DISCOURAGED, FOR I AM YOUR GOD.
> I WILL STRENGTHEN YOU AND HELP YOU. I WILL
> HOLD YOU UP WITH MY VICTORIOUS RIGHT HAND."

God will use His powerful and righteous right hand to wipe our tears, and to gently nudge us on towards the path we should be following. His powerful, loving hands pluck us out of harm's way and bring to us all we need. Put all you need into the loving, caring hands of our Lord and trust Him.

The Bible says, as clay is in the potter's hands, so are we in the Lord's hands. I have a background in pottery from my time as a design major in college. In my pottery classes, I used soft clay on the potter's wheel, which meant my hands would have to be strong and steady, so the pottery would be strong and completely symmetrical. If my hands were off balance in any way, the pottery would not have strength, and it would be vulnerable to breaking.

Like the pottery, God created us to be strong and beautiful in Him. There are no cracks, insecurities, or vulnerabilities that Jesus will not fix.

Today, I want to remind you all that we can put all things into the mighty, righteous right hand of our loving Father! God's arm has not grown too short to reach us wherever we are. He will send help, the help of all of Heaven, to our aid and rescue. He will send angels at our request.

Let us place our burdens in His powerful hands, and cast off our cares to Him.

Revive Us!

DAY 99

The scripture of Psalm 119:25 says:

"I LIE IN THE DUST; REVIVE ME BY YOUR WORD."

I love the message in this scripture. After all, how many of us need revival for our souls?

The definition of revival is "to return to consciousness or life; to become active or flourishing again." God says His Word can revive us. God's Word can strengthen us and breathe new life into us. His Word is alive, and an ever-present help in times of trouble!

The answers we seek are right there in the wonderful pages of the Bible, anointed with His Holy Word. God does not lie! His Word, and every promise, are available to us, His children, through these pages. We can live, move, and have our being in Him.

Let us trust God for His revival in us—and I mean revival by His definition, not ours. God already knows what we need, and He knows when we need it and why we need it! He will never let us down. No, He will never let us be shaken or moved. Trust Him and pray for revival of the soul. We must ask God to show us any cracks and crevices that He longs to heal and revive in our lives.

Let Him refresh you through the power of the blood of Jesus. We are loved so perfectly by our Heavenly Father, and it is time for His refreshing revival to consume us. Seek Him, praise Him, thank Him, and ask Him to refresh and revive you. We have not because we ask not!

The Eagles in My Backyard

DAY 100

My friends, this is a true story, and one that I believe was a prophetic message from God.

It is a very bittersweet story, and yet I believe it is a strong metaphor for what is happening in our world and our nation today. I believe it is a divine word on how we are to receive victory in times of trouble.

A few months ago, my husband and I discovered an eagle's nest high up in the pine tree that comes just over the fence in our backyard. There were three baby eagles: one male and two females. This is highly unusual, as we live in the middle of downtown Houston.

We were so thrilled to find out about these precious baby eagles that we began watching them with binoculars daily. We soon discovered that the youngest was the male eagle, and we started to watch them grow, change, and learn new things.

Often, we saw the mom swoop in, bringing chunks of meat. The baby eagles would be so excited, and would chatter with exuberance every time she came near the nest.

But, then, one day as we were watching, we saw something tragic: when the mom swooped in with food, the baby boy eagle that had never left the nest jumped up with excitement and fell, spiraling out from the very tall pine tree onto the ground. We could not believe it. We witnessed this whole thing in front of our very eyes.

He had fallen into our neighbors' yard, and we could not see him. The neighbors refused to help, calling eagles "nuisances," and, though we were sad, we knew we had to let nature run its course. We just prayed that the mama would somehow rescue her baby eagle.

The very next day, we put a ladder to our fence to see if we could see if the baby had been rescued. We were so sad to see that the baby eagle had been killed by something—it was so devastating!

A few days later, when we investigated the nest, we only saw one baby female and the mom, who was feeding her. Later, in our neighborhood email update, someone shared a picture of the dead baby female eagle on the next street over. It had been hit by a car.

We began praying over our last eagle and the poor mama who seemed so devastated. She would sit in branches and call out, hoping to hear the return call from her babies.

A few days later, as I was sitting in my backyard, I saw the third baby eagle standing in the grass in the middle of my backyard. She was so beautiful and not afraid at all, but then, as my husband and I were watching her, she flew up to sit on our backyard fence. She was sitting there for quite some time, and then she laid down—right there on the fence! Never in my lifetime have I ever seen any kind of bird lay down! We were amazed.

This whole time, I felt like the Lord was talking to me through these eagles, but, at this time, I said to the Lord, "What am I looking at right now? What is this all about?".

And then, as if a sermon were being played out in my mind, I heard the Lord's answer in my spirit, so powerfully.

The Lord told me that the first eagle that fell from the nest died because he was weak, not unlike us, God's people. We will not survive the evil of this world if we are weak, and we need the strength that only comes from the Lord to endure and overcome until the end.

Then, I felt the Lord say the second eagle (that was hit by the car) died because it was distracted by the things of the world. And, like us, when we take our eyes off Jesus, and instead focus on the world, we allow sin and distraction to lord over our lives. We must not let the worldly distractions sway us off the path God has for us. These distractions are strategies of the devil that can destroy us. As the Bible says, many Christians will fall away in the end.

But, then I felt God say that the last eagle, the one that laid down right in front of our eyes, was how we will survive and endure to the end. We, like this eagle, must *rest in Him!*

It is interesting to me that the strongest of the eagles survived because of rest. After this last baby grew and left the nest, we would still see the mom and the baby together occasionally. We hear their calls, as they will sometimes return to the nest, as if to have a reunion. Or, perhaps it is just to join and have a time of rest.

Isaiah 40:31 says:

> "BUT THOSE WHO TRUST IN THE LORD WILL FIND NEW STRENGTH. THEY WILL SOAR HIGH ON WINGS LIKE EAGLES. THEY WILL RUN AND NOT GROW WEARY. THEY WILL WALK AND NOT FAINT."

During these chaotic and uncertain times, we must draw closer to God and strengthen ourselves in Him. We must not be distracted by the evil of this world, but instead keep our focus on our Almighty God. We must simply seek His face and rest; rest in Him as we cast our cares, seek Him daily for his plan. Believe the glory of God will bring a great awakening that will change everything! We will conquer our battles in praises, thanksgiving, and in His rest!

Conclusion

These daily devotions have been a foundation of complete strength and wisdom for me. These are the lessons learned, and the battles fought and won by walking hand-in-hand with the living God. I hope they've encouraged you to live a life of peace and victory by seeking Him first in all things!

I pray these 100 day spent together will strengthen your faith and encourage you daily to live victoriously in Christ Jesus. The word of God is alive, powerful, and when God's promises are declared in faith, abundant victory is our absolute result!

For more inspiration and uplifting content, visit ninaandmichelle.com, and like "Nina Keegan ministries" on Facebook. You can also search your local television listings and YouTube for GRACE GRACE with Nina and Michelle.

> "SEEK THE KINGDOM OF GOD ABOVE ALL ELSE, AND LIVE RIGHTEOUSLY, AND HE WILL GIVE YOU EVERYTHING YOU NEED. SO DON'T WORRY ABOUT TOMORROW, FOR TOMORROW WILL BRING ITS OWN WORRIES. TODAY'S TROUBLE IS ENOUGH FOR TODAY."
>
> MATTHEW 6:33-34

About the Author

Nina's life radically changed 25 years ago, when Jesus became her Lord and Savior. She has since devoted her life to sharing God's message of hope and victory through the grace of His son, Jesus.

After over 10 years of devotional writing for various ministries, including the Christian Broadcasting Network, Nina Keegan became co-host of the popular Christian television show, *Grace Grace with Nina Keegan and Michelle Humphreys*.

Grace Grace is focused on spreading the Gospel through media of magnitude. The show is featured on television networks across the US, Europe, and Africa. Their ministry financially supports orphanage projects across the globe.

With an audience of over 1,000,000 interactions per month, Nina shares the gospel daily on her popular Facebook devotional page, "Nina Keegan Ministries."

Nina is called to be an End Time harvester for God's Kingdom, and to carry out His will, playing her part in His great commission. It is Nina's hope that, through her ministries and powerful testimonies, people's lives will be forever changed. Nina believes that we are all here to play an important role in the advancement of God's kingdom.

Nina Keegan is the mother of two grown sons and a daughter-in-law. She lives with her husband, Richard, in the Houston Area. Nina is the author of *100 Days with God* and *100 Days with God II*.

> "TO GOD BE ALL GLORY IN ALL THINGS.
> APART FROM HIM, WE CAN DO NOTHING."
>
> JOHN 15:5

www.ingramcontent.com/pod-product-compliance
Lightning Source LLC
LaVergne TN
LVHW041542070426
835507LV00011B/876